Grow Smarter

Collaboration Secrets to

Transform Your Income and Impact

Dr. Davia H. Shepherd

An LPL Transformation Series Publication

Green Heart Living Press

Grow Smarter
Collaboration Secrets to Transform Your Income and Impact

An LPL Transformation Series Publication

ISBN (hardback): 978-1-954493-07-0

Cover design by Barb Pritchard

Dedication

To all the bright shining lights that are working their little tail feathers off supporting their communities.

To all the heart-centered entrepreneurs who have a dream that their contribution can help make the world a little bit more beautiful...

I see you. I recognize you. I am you.

Together, we all succeed.

Table of Contents

Acknowledgments

Let me give you a little behind the scenes tour. I cram as much as I can into my days. Without dearest Wayne, my better half, being absolutely amazing, my babies Preston and Christian being such good boys, and without Sandy and Angelica holding things down in the office, it would be impossible to have gotten through this book or anything else for that matter!

Juggling Ladies' Power Lunch (LPL) and our practice is quite the balancing act. I have to make time whenever I can. That's why I had pulled over into the parking lot of a Target while on my way home from work. I pulled over to take a call from Kricket Cody Harrison who was going to be the keynote speaker on our 2020 LPL Fall Summit. Kricket is an outstanding coach and even during our chat, working out logistics of the summit, she managed to plant the seed that has now blossomed into this book.

Once LPL Fall Summit was put to bed, I sat with Elizabeth, our amazing publisher and completely self-imposed a deadline of December 1st to be done with writing this book. Sigh. No one was pushing to get this done, no one even asked me to do this, no one at all, but as Elizabeth Gilbert points out in her book *Big Magic*, inspiration is a real tangible thing.

7

Inspiration for writing this book took hold of me for sure. For the most part the words just poured out. On a couple of occasions when I had a bit of a hiccup I have to say thanks to Elizabeth Hill, Manda Stack, and Robin Finney and truly all my collective spirit sisters for hand-holding when I needed it most.

This book is truly a collaborative effort about collaboration. We recorded 20 episodes of the LPL Show with some of the most heart-centered and amazing female entrepreneurs. All of them are at different stages in business and have different levels of experience using collaboration, and every single interview was gold! Initially I thought that I'd just choose anecdotes from a few of the interviews for inclusion in this work, but there was so much that needed to be shared and I tried to share as much as possible.

I'm so grateful to the women who said yes to being a guest on the LPL show for our limited series *Collaboration Conversations*. Special thank you to Tonia Tyler, Robin Finney, Mary Ann Pack, Teresa Hnat, Dena Otrin, Jackie Baldwin, Tina Forsythe, Prati Kaufman, Tabatha Waters, Suzanne McColl, Susan Trumpler, Carol Tsacoyeanes, Kristi Sullivan, Nadine Mullings, Olympia Hostler, Caili Elwell, Wendy Heller Perotti, Lynn Gallant, and my dear mentor and outstanding friend Darla LeDoux.

I also want to say a special thank you to Chloe

Acknowledgments

White, Mecheal Hamilton, Linda Iovanna, Alyson Griham, and Carleen Limmer.

If I make this too long, y'all will probably get bored and not read the book, and no one wants that, am I right? There just isn't room to thank everyone. Know that I truly appreciate every one of you that touched this project in some way even tangentially.

To my shining stars, the women that make up our Ladies' Power Lunch community. You are the real heroes of this story. You are my inspiration.

Selah

Grow Smarter

Foreword

Wendy Perrotti

When I was in school, I absolutely hated group projects.

There always seemed to be either a bully, a know-it-all, or a freeloader in the mix, and some groups had all three.

Invariably, one or two people would do all the work while everyone else sat on the sidelines. Or even worse, everyone would participate, and the collective compromises would water the outcome down to something so bland that no one was excited about it.

Interestingly, decades later, my kids had the exact same experience.

Group projects are undoubtedly intended to foster collaboration. Unfortunately, they are often assigned without providing the needed skillset to accomplish it. At best the experience is disappointing and at worst, well...

I know I'm not alone in saying that I entered the workforce as an "I'll do it myself" girl.

Of course, life has a way of giving us what we want least and need most.

I landed my first job after college with a national non-profit and quickly rose through the ranks until, at age 26, I held a director-level position.

It was an interesting organization. Every leadership position, from the director-level up to the President had a volunteer counterpart. Every department had a volunteer committee. Virtually every task was undertaken by a combination of paid and volunteer staff.

Essentially, it was a giant "group project" that I had no idea how to navigate. I spent years in committee meetings and board meetings and director's meetings where everybody had an opinion, and no one held the power to make a decision.

Those years made me truly understand the term "death by committee" – we were constantly crafting the mousetrap, but never actually tried to catch a mouse.

I learned a lot.

Soon after I got married, I left that job to join my husband in growing his family business. There was my husband, his brother, their dad, me, and eventually about 50 employees. Collaboration for us meant walking the tightrope between the personal and the professional while trying to create boundaries for our employees that felt warmly familial, unintrusive, and appropriately professional. OY!

Again, I learned a lot.

After about a decade, my husband decided to retire, and I chose to start a boutique coaching and training company. Working alone, it often made sense to team up with a colleague or two for projects, and although I was still a do-it-myself-girl at heart, I was cautiously optimistic at the onset of each collaboration.

Some worked, some didn't, and some were blow-your-mind extraordinary for both my personal development and business outcomes.

Girl, *did I learn a lot!*

Collaboration is woven into every part of our lives. It impacts our personal relationships, our professional outcomes and our sense of fulfillment. And yet the experience most people have is no different than the one they had in high school.

When Dr. Davia asked me to write the forward of this book, I jumped at the chance.

Someone is finally taking the time to collate the best practices of collaboration, so you won't need to suffer quite as many bumps and bruises figuring it out on your own.

While she catalogs some of her own struggles along the path, it's hard to imagine a more natural and dynamic collaborator. Everything Dr. Davia touches flourishes through what looks to the outsider like effortless generosity and sheer fun. And though I believe both are absolutely true of her, she also possesses a ferocious intentionality.

Dr. Davia's five steps of collaboration – ASK, ALIGNMENT, ALL IN, ASSIGNMENT, and APPLICATIONS – provide a welcome (and needed) roadmap that will forever change the way you think about collaboration, enhance the ways you interact with people at every level of your life and, perhaps most importantly, alter the lens you use to view yourself and the world around you.

Dive in, my friends. We are meant to be shining beacons of individual expression and we are meant to do that communally. The magic happens when we learn to collaborate.

Part I

Collaboration Secrets

Butterflies. I'm not sure how they came to be our brand logo and how their spirit and energy came to be infused into everything that I do, but what I can say is that butterflies are a universal symbol of growth, change, and transformation and so they fit in perfectly.

Remember elementary school science class? We learned about the life cycle of the butterfly. I have a couple of books that I read to my six-year-old about that. One is called the impatient caterpillar and that may be one of his favorites. Because of little Christian, I've had to relearn all about the amazing life that is the butterfly. How she starts out as a hungry, hungry caterpillar, eventually settles into her chrysalis, breaks down into a gooey mess and then with the beauty and grace that time allows, she emerges as the beautiful creature that we have come to associate with growth, change, and true transformation.

Isn't that just a metaphor for life though? And as for business, I'm sure we have all experienced our share of growing pains. What I know for sure is that navigating the hungry caterpillar stage in our life and businesses, and even making it out of the chrysalis with ease and grace, can be facilitated when we realize we do not have to ever do this alone and that the collective has our back!

As we were birthing the images that were inspiration for this book, this idea of growing smarter instead of pushing harder to achieve our life goals, even though the butterfly felt like it had to be a part of expressing this idea of growth, what was coming through to me from divine guidance is that we needed to go bigger, that there was more that we had to explore.

Guidance suggested that maybe what we needed was a complete paradigm shift. Perhaps we need to be approaching the idea of growing our businesses and living our optimal lives completely differently, including giving each other more intentional, aligned support. The power of the collective is greater than the sum of her parts.

Every day heart-centered business people work so hard and many struggle to achieve their financial goals. What if more of us embraced these principles? What if more heart-centered entrepreneurs had more resources? It's time to step into the power of our passions and change the world. What if in addition to working our passion we also had the resources to do even more? What if we could expand support for our charities and make a bigger difference?

Barb Prichard, our brand design expert, and I had many ideas that would evoke the message of growing smarter. We thought of the traditional images of growth like a tree, or a seedling, but we realized it has to be so much bigger than that because we are talking about the whole world. We want to make sure the entire world gets the benefit of the heart-centered approach. And then it came to us. Where do worlds grow? In a nebula, of course! In this new paradigm for business growth, growing smarter is the catalyst, the nebula if you will, from which this new world we are creating is being born.

I invite you. Will you join us?

In this section we will talk about:

- Collaborations, what they are and what they are not.

- Why they are AMAZING when they are true collaborations that work well.

- Some true examples of small business collaborations that work.

- What the big guys are up to collaboration-wise.

- How collaborations saved me.

failure to do his part. And then there is the control issue of wanting to "just do everything myself." The belief that if I want something done well I have to do it myself. I mean, who among us hasn't felt that way at some time or another? Trust issues might extend to not feeling comfortable letting others behind the scenes of our businesses, not wanting to open ourselves up to that kind of vulnerability!

There are quite a few other reasons that I have come across and I truly believe that every one of these reasons is valid. And, yet, there is an argument for putting these ideas aside for a moment to consider the pros of collaboration. That list is so long, dear one, that we won't have the time or space to cover all of them here, but let's get a list started? And maybe you can keep adding to this list as more ideas come to you? Awesome.

From Eviction to Millionaire

One of my favorite mentors told us the story once of how she had an eviction notice tacked to her apartment door. This apartment was, of course, where she lived but it also doubled as her office where she met with clients. Through collaborations over a few years, she completely transformed her business and has been able to inspire many with her rags to riches story. She now owns a $50 million business. She tells about how, as a business coach, she formed a collaborative relationship with a financial advisor. They would refer business back and forth all day long. She would send her business clients for financial advice and her partner would send her finance clients over for business advice. Back and forth it went until both women became forces to be reckoned with.

When we get together, suddenly we are working at a level of consciousness where $1+1 > 2$. If you combine your reach with that of your collaboration partner's, together you can achieve explosive growth. The beauty of collaboration is that many of us do many things, but do only a few things very well. If each person plays to her strengths in a partnership, the result is a win. You may have read Napoleon Hill, and you know about the idea of a Mastermind, the exponential increase in knowledge that takes place when two or more minds come together.

More reasons to consider collaboration: It's more fun, you can have bigger visions, big values, and often there is safety in numbers because someone is always there to watch your back. There is more energy, there are more ideas, we learn from each other, and there is an increase in "abundance thinking" when we intentionally work together. What else can you think of? What other reasons can you think of for working together in collaboration?

We need to be having this conversation and thinking about collaboration now more than ever. I've been hosting our private community of women business owners and entrepreneurs for over seven years now, and it's interesting. You get to know people reasonably well. You get to know people's concerns and what the commonalities are, and one thing I hear often from a lot of women is they are not making the income they want and they are not touching nearly as many lives as they might have hoped when they dared dream of doing the thing they are doing to make the world a better place.

The problem is that many women that ditched their 9-5 to lean into their passion, have had their passion become their 24/7. Somehow their expectations of success were different from what is presenting before them now. And they are tired and they don't know what the next step is.

Most of the women I talk to who mention these kinds of concerns are powerhouses in the true sense of the word. They aren't just sitting back waiting for life to happen to them, y'all. You would never call them lazy. Every single day they are working on their businesses and IN their businesses. In the best way they know, they are working HARD. Some achieve modest success, but many struggle quite a bit, and very few break that glass ceiling of outstanding, abundant success.

Think about it. You know what I'm saying is 100% true. But don't just take my word for it. I have stats, y'all, from: *Forbes*, American Express OPEN, and from the National Association of Women Owned Businesses. In America, women own about 11.6 million firms but only 4.2% of all women-owned firms enjoy revenue of $1M or more. REVENUE! I'm not even talking about personal income here. We are talking about total revenue.

I know a few thousand of these women who own small businesses, and while some of them do not have goals that are that lofty, they all share something in common: They put in their time. If they have come from corporate and have started their own business, they work harder at it than they ever have before. These women work late nights and weekends, while still taking care of all their other responsibilities. Like champions, they are taking care of household responsibilities, children, sometimes aging parents or other family members, and, of course, still making time to nurture and support their life partners. These women are golden, these women are me, these women are you, and these women are ready to explore another way.

Most of them have done all the things: hired a business coach, changed their mindsets, networked their little hearts out, set up websites, and SEO'd themselves to exhaustion. They have email lists as long as Santa's; they have social media presences that major corporations would envy; they have chased all the bright shiny objects that promised growth of their business, and they have learned so much along the way...but when it comes down to it, you know, down to dollars and cents, in the whole world scheme of things, they make a little, they get a little recognition, but somehow the big dollars remain elusive.

These women will tell you with heartfelt honesty that they are not in it for the money. They are not wrong. That's commendable, in a way. But here's the thing that they all know for sure. They sure could use a few more days off, a couple more vacations, the ability to hire more staff to support them. They know that the more they make the more they can support the people they believe that they are sent here to support. The more they make the more they can do in their communities and the more they make the more they can give back! And, just maybe, maybe the more they make the better the world becomes for all of us? I believe so.

One such woman is Raquel. I think you might relate to her story because I know a lot of women just like her. She is a hard worker. She had what many would call a pretty enviable position in corporate America. She was a top producer and her higher ups were sad to see her go. With her gone, they could kiss their bonuses goodbye!

She left the corporate world to share her gifts and talents, talents that supported one of the well-known blue chip companies, with small business owners. She was excited. She did her market research because she's just that kind of type A person. She invested in the best technology, marketing, and support staff. While she did see some return on her investment, she was working so many hours per day that her health suffered. I spoke to her just this week and, for health reasons, she is taking a break from her business and is even considering a part-time job just to cover expenses while she recovers. This is an extreme case but not unusual and not too unlike my very own story, but we will get to that later.

There's also a necessity for businesses to be agile during changing times. Many of us have blueprints that we have been following to grow our businesses. These methods may have worked for a while but as things change, many of us find that those guidelines no longer work in the environment that is now. Suddenly everyone is "pivoting" up a storm. But pivoting to where and into what, and what guarantees of success do we have?

A very smart person (the identity of which is a mystery), once suggested that "the definition of insanity is doing the same thing and expecting different results." I tend to agree. Trying the same old strategies that provided, at best, mediocre results, and focusing on these as our core business strategies during changing times... INSANITY!

Once upon a time, there were two real estate agents who met in a networking meeting. Instead of the traditional: "We do the same thing so we can't possibly support each other," they actually decided to become partners.

One of the first properties they ended up listing turned out to be a part of a large estate. Some super rich person had died and there were additional properties as well as a ton of high priced stuff that needed to be disposed of. The executor was so impressed by their work ethic and their ability to work together that he entrusted them with the entire estate.

Today, these two small town realtors are big city auction house owners and they are now considered the go-to team when it comes to getting your fine pieces sold over here in our neck of the woods. The point of this is that they couldn't have seen the opportunity that was coming, but through the power of collaboration they paved the way for great impact and great income.

OK, you are starting to warm up to this idea of collaborating. I can tell. You want to know more about the anatomy of great collaborations, you want to know more about overcoming what holds us back from amazing collaborations, and you want to know the five steps to going from alone in your business to exponential abundance.

What's a Collaboration?

Pull up a chair dear one. You are in the right place. The water's fine...dive right in.

I'm going to invite you to remember elementary school biology! I know. Middle school brings back bad memories for the majority, but I'm sure that, like me, science class was your bright spot... no? That's just me? Cool. Good to know. You know how you probably thought you would never need to know this in the real world when you were all grown up? If I can prove you wrong, then my work here is done!

Anywhooo... I know you remember that lesson you learned about the different types of relationships between animals out in the wild. If not, here's a refresher.

The exciting predator/prey relationship: I expend a tremendous amount of energy to hunt you, I eat you, then thank goodness there are lots of you because I've got to go find another one like you and do it all over again.

Symbiosis: Lots of different ways that this plays out and we will dive a little more into this. The bottom line is that you and me, we are most likely nothing like each other, but we form a close relationship of sorts.

Competition: This one assumes finite resources and, in the end, just like in *The Highlander*, there can only be one... (Nothing? Crickets? That's cool.)

OK, you are thinking, 'Thanks for the primer on

elementary biology and for the reminder about that great show I used to watch back in elementary school.' (It's *Highlander* guys, how does no one remember this?)

But I know you are itching to learn what this has to do with growing and scaling your business, your income, your influence, and your impact. Here it is: The majority of successful organisms living on the planet (humans included) find themselves in the symbiosis camp at some point in their life cycle. TRUE STORY. As for humans, if you think about it, collaboration is something we learn from early on in life. Most functioning family units use the concept of collaboration to achieve the family goals. These seemingly simple things perhaps lay the foundation for us to consider collaboration as a part of a functioning society.

So, maybe there is something we can learn from this for our businesses?

If you think like a predator in your business, you are like a hapless, sleazy used car salesman. Somehow he always is the butt of analogies everywhere, and if you are a legitimate used car salesman, then this is obviously not about your wonderful self. Deal? We are envisioning a predator/prey relationship. Think of a spider and fly. The salesman lies in wait for the customer, traps her in his web, and consumes her. She buys what he's into this science stuff and being able to relate it to biz is ringing all my bells. But I'm bringing it back to growing our businesses. I know for you ecology nerds out there that I am over simplifying things but what do you want from me? I'm a biochemistry nerd; I just have the basics on this stuff!!

So, onwards to symbiosis. We can break this down into three basic categories. There's mutualism, commensalism, and parasitism. Don't grab for your pillows yet, it's about to get exciting.

In a business partnership you can have a case of Win – Win – Win: That's mutualism. Everyone wins! It's just unicorns, rainbows, and butterflies all day long. This brings to mind the case of my favorite example of a collaboration gone right. One of my beloved mentors who is a business coach would refer clients to her financial advisor collaborator who would also at a similar rate refer business right back to her. She won, her collaboration partner won, the clients won. Everyone's business grew in impact and in income, and the clients, well, they won, too. They got a richer experience, got exposed to additional resources, and they were able to grow their businesses, too. The ripple effect is still being felt today from that collaboration. I was so impressed by it that it may have changed my life, and now I'm writing about it in a book... Crazy good!

You can have a case of Lose - Lose: That's how I

think of parasitism. Some think of it as Win-Lose but I do not and here's why: For a while, the one party wins while clearly harming the other, and then eventually the other business can never reach its full potential so the resources available for that good-for-nothing parasite are still limited.

Recently, I was interviewing a dear friend on the LPL Show, our highly acclaimed Ladies' Power Lunch podcast and YouTube show, and she told me about an experience that she had with collaboration that was less than ideal. I think this is an outstanding example of Lose-Lose. My friend is the princess of collaborations, and she embarked upon a collaboration with a group of women. Venues were rented, deposits were paid, and preparations were made for the big day. Everything was in her name, and all the deposits were out of her pocket. At the last minute, one of her collaborators dropped out for what seemed to be no good reason, after benefiting from the promotion of her business through the event. My friend was left with all the expenses and the need to fill her collaboration partner's spot at the last minute.

This was a great experience... for learning. She, and by extension all of us, can look at this scenario, pick it apart, and figure out all the things that we should avoid when collaborating going forward. We should have things in writing when commingling funds, we should have contingency plans because nothing ever goes 100% the way we planned... The most important lesson in this is: Let us, when we are collaborating, be all in. Let us have our word be our bond, let us be there for our collaboration partners, and may we never leave them in the lurch.

And then there is the Win – "Eh" relationship. That's how I'm defining commensalism. One person in the partnership is doing fine with or without the partner and the other one is just kind of benefiting from the relationship but not contributing anything of real value to the joining. Let me get National Geographic on you and give you an example from nature. There are a lot of animals that some predators have no interest in eating. (Someone should look more closely into that, maybe speak to the manager? Karen, are you on that?) Some of these animals follow the predator around, from a safe distance, and then after the predator is done with its snack, and off on the next adventure, the commensal swoops in and cleans up for the Win. The predator doesn't really care anything about what the commensal is up to, but the commensal is having a party with not too much effort.

When it comes to business, I'm sure you can think of examples, but what comes to mind for me are businesses that use the model of getting clients through the efforts of others. I think of the ambulance-chasing lawyer of lore. They hang back in the cut, and once the health care has been handled, they take care of the legal issues. I know there is some negative connotation here, just because of society and stereotypes, but for the most part the client wins because she doesn't have to go searching for the services that she needs, the services come to her, and the emergency health care workers are neither harmed nor advantaged by this.

Another business model comes to mind for me. Please humor me, I am in the healthcare field so it is no wonder my examples are leaning this way. I observed a medical practice many years ago. The practice was primarily an OB-GYN practice, focused on women's health but they had a couple of pediatricians as part of their practice. As I think about it now, it seems genius, and I wonder why more pediatricians don't work in this way. The pregnant mothers would have an opportunity to meet the pediatricians long before they ever had their babies. For all my first time mothers out there, having a health care practitioner sit with you and allay your fears is priceless. Then, the pediatrician would also come to meet the new moms and the baby in the hospital! Instant new patient. In this case, the OB-GYN practice could continue on easily without a pediatrician, but having one or two on staff certainly benefited the pediatricians and, might I say, also the end client, the moms and babies.

I see the idea of symbiosis as analogous to collaboration. The continuum of collaboration can range from networking or a referral relationship to a full on formalized partnership. Utilizing models that prioritize working synergistically exist in nature, and those models work in business, too. Don't just take my word for it. Let's take a look at how some of our favorite larger corporations have used collaborations to make millions, and what we as agile small businesses can learn from the behemoths.

Chapter Review

Let's personalize this for you and your business.

1) When you think of competition and your business, what comes to mind?

2) What business model are you currently using? Predator? Some form of symbiosis? Competition?

3) How is the business model you are using currently working for you? Is there room for growth or improvement? In what way?

just do not have enough space here to go through every episode. They were all soooo good, but I want to highlight a few that offered specific lessons that we all can learn from.

The first one that I want to share is the interview that I had with our amazing guest Wendy Heller Perrotti.

I love chatting with this lady! From the very first time we met at a networking event where she was the speaker, I adored her energy, and we became friends. Let me tell you a little bit about her to kind of set the stage for how our conversation unfolded.

So, my girl Wendy is a master coach, y'all! She is also a leadership trainer and reinvention guru. She is one of the people that I interviewed that I'm truly able to say is an expert. She has been at this for a while now. For over 25 years, she has helped thousands of individuals and organizations create change that sticks. She has also had to make her own changes in her own life. If you chat with her she will tell you all about how she, in her "first life," traveled the country from disaster to disaster as a national media spokesperson for the American Red Cross. You can see how that would be stressful. She left that behind to spend more time at home with her kids and became what we like to call a serial entrepreneur.

Wendy is a BOSS! She was able to initially build a

multi-seven figure business with her husband, which they both found DID NOT light them up. Can you imagine? You find yourself hitting the financial goals but find that you are not being personally fulfilled? She ended up leaning into her passion, and again, because she is a true genius, created multiple six-figure coaching businesses "using hard science to teach the soft skills required for real change, " as she puts it. If you ever want to reach out to her, I'd say start by listening to her podcast, A *Glimpse Inside - Moving people from stuck to happy*; or hop on over to her website: www.wendyperrotti.com.

Wendy and I had a grand time chatting away about collaboration because, like me, she is a big proponent of using collaboration to grow business. She jokingly says, "I've had so many collaborations! Some have changed my life and others, let's say, have been learning experiences!"

I can honestly say I feel exactly the same way. What stands out is that she brought a really interesting perspective to this conversation about collaboration. She tells the story about a collaboration that she did when she just started her one-on-one coaching business. She admits, and I know many of us can relate to this, that it was a challenge to build a practice from scratch. This is where it gets good. She used the power of collaboration to solve her dilemma. To maintain her income goals, together with a colleague, she developed another project doing corporate work while she built her private practice.

What is that sweet spot between casual collaboration and full-on partnership, and how can a simple contract make all the difference? Wendy mentions that when she was entering into this particular collaboration, she didn't want a business partner. Both she and her collaboration partner wanted to own their own coaching practices and not consolidate into a partnership. They weren't sure it would be a long-term arrangement. They both were sure they wanted to work together and so they came up with a novel solution. They set up their collaboration in the same way that you would set up a brand. She and her colleague called in an attorney to set up a very simple contract. They were able to do a lot of work together and it was a beautiful collaboration which continues in some form to this day. They thought outside of the box and still managed to meet all the needs that they had at the time.

An interesting point that came out of our conversation is that they had to learn how to work with each other during that collaboration. Generally when we are outlining the must do's for a collaboration, one of the first things people think of is the importance of communication. It's true, communication is important for collaboration to work, but what does that even mean? I asked Wendy and she explained a little more detail of her story. It turns out that she and her partner are polar opposites. One of her #1 must-haves for collaboration is having similar if not identical values. The values push the direction of the collaboration. She and her colleague have incredibly similar values, but other than that, they have different personalities, backgrounds, etc.

Wendy likes the big picture while her partner is very linear in her thinking. She explained that this caused problems for them at first, but because they had amazing communication (filled with love and humor) they were successful. She says that learning how to communicate with each other around their differences was a huge key to their success. She recommends leaning into your communication style and communicating in a way that your partner is able to hear you. It also can't be one-sided; the other partner has to do the same. Maybe that is what opens the door to the amazing collaborations. She also notes that both have to come to the collaboration with an openness to having the hard conversations. It just takes one person who is able to bring up the tough points with an objective voice, love, and understanding, accompanied by openness on the part of the other to hear and listen. From there success can be achieved.

Her words of wisdom for those on the fence about collaboration: Start small. If you are thinking of collaborating with someone, do something small together, see how you work with each other. Make sure the collaboration is going to work.

She also suggests:

1) Make sure your values are aligned.

2) Be true to who you are.

3) Be open and allow your collaborators to do the same.

4) Be crystal clear on the intended mission and outcome of   the collaboration.

5) Hold yourself and others accountable for #4.

6) Trust your gut and move on if it gets stuck or is a bad fit; she is emphatic on this point.

And finally, she makes a point that I think we should consider in all areas of our lives. If you're going to collaborate with someone you already know, don't expect them to behave differently in the collaboration than they do in other areas of their life or business. Consider if they've had a hard time staying focused, finishing things, following up, being on time, staying accountable, etc...

The next interview that I thought was incredibly valuable in its takeaways was with one of my favorite mentors, Darla LeDoux.

What Small Business Successes Have to Teach Us

I bonded with Darla over the fact that we both left the science field to become coaches. I like to say I'm a recovering researcher, and she describes herself as a recovering engineer. Darla has had a lot of experience coaching and certifying retreat leaders and transformational coaches. Let me give you her 411. She is an outstanding business coach, she has been my coach for some time now, and, to be completely transparent, she's completely changed the trajectory of my business. One of my first interactions with her was when I was several years into leading retreats and losing money on EVERY SINGLE ONE. I was scouting retreat locations online and, somehow, through tracking cookies or something like that on the internet, her book, *Retreat and Grow Rich*, kept following me around from webpage to webpage. I obviously had to purchase it. From reading her book, I started listening to her podcast and the rest is history. Since then, I've been a guest on her podcast, the same one I used to listen to such a long time ago. I was so pleased to have her as a guest presenter at our recent LPL Summit and to have her on the LPL Show for Collaboration Conversations.

If you ask Darla what she does, she will tell you that she is "co-creating a world in which transformational work is the norm, and where each person's intuitive magic is valid, valued, and visible." I love that and because of her I'm no longer *as afraid*

(I'm still a little nervous, y'all) of sharing my significant intuitive gifts with patients, clients, and the world. I still have work to do in this regard but if you had met me pre-Darla you would be talking to a completely different woman!

Our conversation on the show was particularly instructive because we focused on when collaboration is a *bad* idea? Darla shared stories about collaborations that did not go well. Seems counterintuitive maybe but I feel that it is from these stories that sometimes we learn the most.

Darla thinks of collaboration as pooling resources, considering the idea of how does your gift support my gift? When resources and connections are pooled we are able to have a better impact. When you are part of a collaboration, you don't have to do everything yourself – it is sort of like the concept of working smarter. And as for the clients, they have a richer experience.

When I asked Darla what her experience has been with collaboration she responded that her results have been mixed. She has seen a lot of what works but she has seen a lot of what doesn't work, also. One such type of collaboration that does not work is what she refers to as transactional collaborations. These collaborations are based on the agreement of, "You do this for me; I'll do this thing for you." If it's like that, she says, it can feel forced and yucky and in the end no one comes out of it feeling as though they have been treated fairly. Such a collaboration is especially ill-fated if values are not aligned. Just like Wendy said, again it comes to the fore that having shared values is super important.

Darla gave the example of her client, Kate, who hosted a retreat. Kate was a yoga instructor, and she had her collaboration partner come in as a presenter for a portion of the retreat. That seems fine on the surface; however, for months prior to the retreat, Kate worked her bum off and was the one making all the investments of time and finances. They were supposed to be equal partners but Kate was the one who ended up booking everything, working on the planning of the retreat for months, marketing the retreat, and filling all the slots. She did well, she was all in. She had done all the work, and her partner received half of the proceeds. In my opinion a situation like this would be a classic example of a parasitic relationship.

Another way that she has seen collaborations go wrong has been when people use collaborations to hide. For example, if two people are working together to host an event, and there is no explicit conversation at the beginning, and each person assumes the other person is going to fill the event, it can end up not getting sold at all. When each person is waiting for the other person to do something, then nothing happens. In situations like this, Darla says the energy of the collaboration is just not being aligned. If you are coming from a hiding energy your collaboration will not work.

Her previous example was of a client's collaboration experience that went poorly, but she has had her own failed collaborations which she was kind enough to share with us. She mentioned in particular two collaborations that went poorly. One was a collaboration to create a retreat for teen girls that didn't actually happen, and the other was a collaborative event tour that she planned with a group of retreat leaders that got mixed results.

Darla did a retreat tour in five different cities called the "Simply Powerful" tour. In each of the cities she co-led a retreat with one local woman. It was a lot of work and very tiring. The results in each city varied depending on who the collaborator was. Darla points out that she made the investments financially, she placed the ads, she worked to fill the events, her team did the marketing. She also admits that she did not create any agreements that each woman would bring a certain number of people, so the attendance varied wildly from five people in one city to over 30 in others. The experiences were vastly different depending on the effort that her partner put in.

Darla really did open up with us on this one, and I am so grateful for her vulnerability. In analyzing the results of these events she was able to pick up on patterns that she has had since childhood. She realized that she always approaches everything with an "I'll do it attitude." She developed that to support her mom who was very overwhelmed with life. When we aren't keeping our energy clear, if we have old agreements that we are committed to, we can easily bring those attitudes to and unwittingly sabotage our partnerships. In this situation, Darla suggests that she was so committed to always being the one to shoulder the burden that she did not take the time to outline the parameters of the collaboration.

We often think that a failed collaboration is caused by someone not pulling their weight, but being the one who always does everything can also be detrimental. Like Darla, I tend to be a doer. I was the one who would just complete the school group project by myself for fear of others not doing their portion, or not doing it well enough. This conversation with Darla was a huge "Aha!" moment for me.

My biggest takeaways from our interview with Darla? What's important here? What is it that we need to learn?

- The energy that you bring to a collaboration needs to be the energy of being all in and being ready to do everything that is possible. Being very clear about our commitment and being willing to rise to the occasion.

- Explicit conversations have to be had with the partner at the beginning. Clarity about each member's responsibilities needs to be outlined.

- We have to check on the old patterns of behavior that we bring to our collaborations. Our patterns can get in the way of us hearing suggestions and receiving support and being open to the available opportunities.

- We need to have a soul conversation: asking ourselves if this is a truly aligned partnership. Trust our intuition and hear it loud and clear.

- We need to be energetically aligned with our pricing, understand our value, and not suffer in silence.

- We need to be open and upfront as we make decisions about finances and never let the money conversations go by the wayside.

- Be creative and present with each other's energy, be practical. Be more fluid and be open to receive, and open to support.

We truly do learn a lot when things do not go exactly as planned.

Teresa Hnat is an outstanding photographer. She specializes in brand photography and videography and she says that her goal is to create stunning visuals that help you stand out and shine. That is absolutely true. Almost every time I see her photos I recognize her aesthetic sense. She is a talent to be reckoned with. Teresa is actually new to her entrepreneurial journey but during our conversation she shared so many nuggets.

Teresa is a lovely, soft spoken person with a tremendous talent and genuine kindness. During our interview, she was very open with us, for which we are truly grateful. She shared about one of the great collaborations that she has with another of our LPL members, copywriter Caili Ellwell. What I most want to share with y'all is the story she told about the time she collaborated with a hairdresser.

The plan was that the hairdresser would create some highly artistic, funky, creative hairstyles for Teresa's portfolio, and then some more traditional hairstyles for her own portfolio. And, Teresa would photograph all the hairstyles for each of the portfolios. Of course, Teresa, the giving person that she is, fulfilled her side of the bargain and photographed the regular hairstyles for the hairdresser. Unfortunately, the hairdresser never designed those funky and artistic hairstyles for Teresa's portfolio. When Teresa reached out to schedule her shoot, the hairdresser put her off.

At first glance it may seem that Teresa's collaboration partner was just terrible and not living up to her end of the bargain. But, Teresa explained that there was more to the story. Teresa shared that sometimes we are people pleasers and in our effort to make others happy we may be too afraid to say what it is that we want or to follow-up repeatedly. We don't want to rock the boat and seem needy. And so we allow ourselves to be railroaded.

She emphasizes that before getting into a collaboration we need to be able to express our goals and intentions. Communication is key as is confidence. We need to work on self-confidence, work on our confidence in our work product, and our business before hopping into a collaboration. As far as the hairdresser collaboration goes, her lack of confidence prevented her from following up and having her needs met in the partnership.

My big takeaways from our conversation:

- Be sure to communicate all the details in the beginning, maybe even getting counsel involved.

- Develop the confidence in your ability to do your job and confidence to speak up for your needs.

- Schedule ongoing meetings for ongoing collaborations preferably ahead of time.

- Know that sometimes the energy is not right, sometimes the timing is not right; it's OK to say, "No, Thank You!"

- Consider: Does the collaboration align with your values? If no, then it's a firm "No."

- Be sure to, as much as possible, have a plan of action not just a goal, and be sure that both people are on track.

- Create an effective content management system.

Chapter Review

Let's personalize this for you and your business.

1) What are your biggest takeaways from these small business stories?

2) What can you apply to your business?

3) Are there any areas where you could improve your communication with your collaboration partners or potential partners?

4) What are your values in your business? Which ones are non-negotiable when it comes to collaboration?

5) How are you able to tune in to the energy of a potential collaboration? How can you be more aware of your intuition and the role it can play?

Meditation

Close your eyes and imagine that you are heading to your destination at the end of a long river. You are swimming along this gentle flowing river. Take a deep breath and imagine that you can feel the gentle support of the water as it carries you along. The water is gentle, relaxing, cool, clear, and supportive. As you float on by, you realize you are traveling along at a speed greater than any vehicle along the shore. You are being carried swiftly, safely, and surely downstream with no extra or extreme effort on your part. Enjoy the feel of being supported almost weightlessly, notice how wonderfully and quickly you are making it to your destination as you are with the flow. Take a deep breath in and imagine that you have arrived at your destination.

1) What came up for you during this visualization?

2) Was there any resistance to flow?

3) Were there any concerns that popped into your mind as you imagined swimming along with a flowing river?

4) What metaphors do you think this may be for the way you approach collaborations?

Grow Smarter

Chapter 4

What Big Name Collaborations Have to Teach Us

When I think of the big guns, the big companies that are known for their collaboration success, my favorites are Apple, Hewlett Packard, Microsoft, Ben and Jerry's, and Disney.

I've mentioned that I'm a recovering researcher, and I may also have mentioned that I'm coming from the pharmaceutical field. In pharma, there are no strangers to collaborations, though in many cases it's more of a takeover. I remember when I was with one company that was working on a particular drug, and our scientists had the biochemistry and chemistry piece on lock! Just thinking about it, I get excited because the science on this drug was amazing, but guess what we didn't have? A delivery system that worked. Look, y'all, if you have a cure but you can't get it to where you need it to work, you've got nothing. Fortunately, the powers that be in the company were open to and welcomed the idea of collaboration. They partnered with another big name pharma company that had physicists who came up with an out-of-the-box delivery method, one we frankly had thought about but couldn't execute. Who was the big winner in all this? The patients! With amazing scientists working together, they got a cure that wouldn't have shown up otherwise. That's the power of collaboration.

Many other big businesses provide outstanding case studies for collaboration, however, I've singled out these ones for the lessons they provide for us in small business. Of course, since this is a collaborative project, I polled our Ladies' Power Lunch members and asked them what big name collaborations they liked best, and I got a lot of fun ones, too: Ringling Brothers and Barnum and Bailey, Alex and Ani, Colgate and Palmolive. Who knows S&H Green Stamps? If we are talking about collaborations between celebrities of sorts, how about Oprah and Deepak Chopra or Penn and Teller? And then, of course, there were the LPL comments that made me smile widely, maybe even LOL: Laurel and Hardy, Laverne and Shirley.

A Tale of Two Steves

Apple has become such a textbook case of collaboration. There are, obviously, things that could have gone better to make for an even better outcome but what I want to focus on here is what worked for these guys, why it worked, and how we can apply it to our small businesses for growth. Back in 1976, the story goes that a couple of guys named Steve

What Big Name Collaborations Have to Teach Us

(Wozniak and Jobs) and a guy named Ronald Wayne founded Apple Computer, Inc. Everything I have read, listened to, or watched about the Apple story suggests that these guys started out as friends. Wayne dropped out of the partnership pretty early on and the partnership between the Steves didn't last more than a few years, but what they created together changed the way we do, well, everything and has secured them a page in the history books forever.

If you do not own an Apple product, I'm going to go out on a limb here and say that Apple still manages to touch your life in some way. From the devices, to the software products, to the online platforms like iTunes, to all kinds of applications and services. A little collaboration that apparently started in someone's garage is now legendary.

So, what was so great about them? Wozniak was brilliant and built things; to start with the Apple 1. And then there was that other Steve. Well, he had a vision. Legend has it that he could see how computers, which back then were huge things that took up rooms and rooms of space, would one day be in every home. I'm not sure if he could see how pervasive computers would become from back then. If I count the computers in my home I can truthfully say that between laptops, tablets, smart watches, and phones... well, that's a lot of computers. I even have two computers here on my office desk as I write in my office: my laptop and my iPhone. It seems so obvious now but back then it was anything but.

What can we take away from their partnership? Look, y'all, to be honest, I wasn't there in the room with these guys, but I'm pretty sure that for their collaboration to have lasted as long as it did, and, in order for it to have been successful, they had to all have a pretty good idea of what they wanted individually from a collaboration. For us as small business owners, I think that has to be the first step. We are best served when we are able to know what it is that we want. Know yourself before we do anything else, including joining with another.

There is significant evidence that the Steves were buddies back in the day. They were friends in high school and both were aligned in their desire to create computers. Shared goals, shared values, even if the collaboration partners have their genius focused in different areas, is priceless.

There is the aspect of commitment. How committed do you think the Steves were to their project? From everything I've ever seen about both Steve Jobs and Wozniak, I would surmise that they were both all-in as far as their collaboration went.

One of the keys to their success, in my opinion, would have to be the fact that they mastered the art of assignment. So many times, partners come together and forget that each person brings their special gifts and talents to the table. In the case of Apple, each member of the collaboration contributed from their genius. They focused on their strengths, the thing that they were amazing at, and the partnership was most successful as a result.

In our interview with Wendy Perrotti, she talks a little bit about a collaboration that she had that went on much too long. I think that one of the biggest lessons that we can learn from the example of Apple may not be what you think. My biggest takeaway is that it's OK to try a collaboration, and it is OK for a collaboration not to last forever.

The amazing collaboration that spawned a brave new world in technology in the form of Apple did not last very long but had tremendous impact. What is more important than the length of the collaboration is what impact did it have while it existed? What benefits did you receive while it existed? What lessons are you able to take away from the experience?

Wendy advises us to start small with our collaborations, and she suggests that it's super important to know when to call it quits. Setting up an amicable exit strategy at the beginning if things hit the skids is always a wise course of action, y'all. Just saying.

Bill and Dave and Lu's Excellent Adventure

The story of Hewlett Packard is probably less famous than the Apple example but it is one that you will find in many a textbook. Hewlett Packard is another tech company that has changed the face of the world as we know it. Let's examine what it has to teach us entrepreneurs.

While preparing the content of this book, I was up late one night writing. I looked at the clock and saw that it was 3:30 am. I had a 7 am start to my day, so briefly reading back what had poured through me, I gave it my stamp of approval, thought it was pretty darn good, shut down my computer, and went to bed.

When I logged back on to continue telling the stories, wouldn't you just know, the gold I spent hours typing was nowhere to be found! Completely missing, and I kept asking myself where did it go and, more importantly, will I be able to recreate the magic that I felt I had on the page the first time around? I reached out to one of my dear friends and coaches, Robin Finney. (You can see my interview with her on *Collaboration Conversations*.) What came out of my brief coaching conversation with her was also pure gold, and so I'm going to again tell the story of Bill and Dave and the amazing company they built, but I'm going to tell it from a different perspective, and interject a little of my own story here.

What Big Name Collaborations Have to Teach Us

The Hewlett Packard company, founded in 1939, changed the face of technology, providing computer hardware, software, and services to government and big business, as well as to small to midsize business and household consumers. If you check any website or any textbook, you will see the story of how two engineers, Bill Hewlett and David Packard, started their company in a one-car garage in Palo Alto, California, the building that now is designated the "Birthplace of Silicon Valley."

We all love a good "rags to riches story," and while I wouldn't go so far as to say they came from rags, I'd say their humble beginnings provide inspiration for us all. Almost every solopreneur can relate to the story of serving every function in a business: from janitor, to customer service, to the actual provider of the service or product that the business is known for. The story of Hewlett Packard is similar where they admit to doing almost everything in their business in the early days.

Before I dive into my personal take on how we can use their examples of collaboration in our businesses, let's see if this big biz collaboration checks all the boxes for what we have established as being the pillars of an outstanding collaboration. From everything I've read about this famous Bill and Dave, they come across as careful and thoughtful planners. They are well known for never biting off more than they could chew. One of the first pillars of a good collaboration is starting with one's self and determining what is wanted from coming together with another. From all the research, it does appear that these luminaries had that piece on lock.

As far as alignment goes it appears that both partners were friends first and that there was no ego interfering with their partnership. Some sources even mention that they tossed a coin to see whose name would go first in their company name. What was important for them were their shared values and the product they were driven to bring to the world. And as for all-in and assignment, the work ethic of both men is the story of legends. Each partner focused on their area of expertise. Bill Hewlett was an engineer who excelled at circuit technology, and David Packard knew all about the manufacturing process. With each partner focusing on his particular area of expertise, it is no wonder that orders started pouring in. By 1965, just under 30 years after their business started with an initial investment of $538.00, they saw sales of $165 million.

So, check and double check! HP makes the grade for me as a company worthy of recognition for its successful collaboration. However, I want to take this one a little further and introduce the idea that we have all kinds of collaborations in our lives, those that are formal and obvious and those that are not as obvious. Most of the media that discusses the example of HP does not mention another collaborator that I think deserves a round of applause. I believe also that for so many of us as entrepreneurs we may take for granted the role of collaboration that our family plays in the whole mix.

Let us talk a little bit here about Lucile Packard. We don't see her name on the company logo but I would argue, and David Packard does explain in great detail in his book *The HP Way*, that her contribution, though behind the scenes, was significant.

Lu is, in my opinion, a remarkable example for all of us as women. She was an English major from Stanford back when women attending Stanford was not a thing. When she and Dave got married, she provided her whole-hearted support for the business endeavor that was HP. There are stories of her supporting the family on her $90 per month paycheck so the team could focus on doing the work. She did a lot of the behind-the-scenes work too! She says that her role was: "Typing the letters, keeping the records, and heating up the coffee pot." She is described as the laundress, housekeeper, breadwinner, company hostess, etc...

How many of us as entrepreneurs can relate to having the support of our collaboration partners, whether it be our spouse, other family members, or friends? These are some of the unsung heroes of our stories, and I do believe that this kind of collaboration deserves special mention.

That leads me to share my personal story. The story of me going from alone and in debt in my business to being debt-free and using collaboration to grow at every turn features a similar hero to Lu. My dear husband was so understanding when I had my crisis of conscience and tearfully outlined to him why I had to go from earning my six-figure salary to working directly with patients and going back to school.

His steadfast support was what got me through the tough times, and when I had no income from our business he took care of us as a family. When we were short on cash flow in my business on so many occasions he floated us a "loan." When we had maxed out our lines of credit, he was the one who stepped in and helped out with that, too, and who used his accounting expertise to help us get back on sound footing.

He was a constant fixture at our open houses, always helping with odd jobs around the office such as painting, and juggling things with children to accommodate me attending all the early morning and late night networking events. He did all that and more, and continues to be the reason I can do what I do.

Sometimes when I talk to newly-minted entrepreneurs, I hear complaints about the fact that often friends and family do not support their businesses by purchasing their widgets. That's true a lot of the time, but as a firm believer that what we focus on expands, I would like to invite us to tune in to our own lives. How many times have family or friends "collaborated" with us in some way so that we could advance our entrepreneurial dream? We don't do it alone, and it's always important to acknowledge not just some, but all of the collaborations that have helped us along the way.

To close out this section I'd like to mention Prati Kaufman, marketing guru and classic example of a genius when it comes to collaborations. In our interview on LPL Collaboration Conversations, she confirms this idea of considering friends and family as our collaboration partners. She cites that in her case, in addition to the non-financial support, her friends and family have contributed as actual investors in her business. She wisely says that her business is successful because her friends and family have a stake in it. When pressed to explain further she adds, "I think of my family as having equal stakes in my business. They give me advice, they do everything!"

The alignment with Prati and her family is clear, just like Bill and Dave were in alignment and were all in. Each focused on their strengths, and with the support of Lu, provided us with a stellar example to follow that checks all the boxes for an outstanding collaboration.

Microprocessors and Software, Oh My!

It may seem at first glance that we are only highlighting tech companies as our case studies here, but it's just the way the cookie crumbled and was not particularly orchestrated to be that way. I feel as though we can't talk about collaboration in business without at least giving cursory inspection to what made tech giant Microsoft the force it is to be reckoned with today.

Looking at the early days of Bill Gates and Paul Allen getting together, one theme that has run through our examples pops up here again. Bill and Paul had been friends since they were kids. They knew each other, there was a certain level of trust in their capabilities and ability to work together, and they both had a clear vision of what they wanted from a partnership.

Both were skilled in computer programming and they worked together to be innovative. So very often amazing ideas come about when more than one mind bellies up to the table. This was no exception. Back then, most computers were huge things that took up rooms of space. New devices called microcomputers were being developed, and the duo of Bill and Paul had the brilliant idea to apply a programming language commonly used for the huge computers to these newfangled microcomputers. Both partners came together to develop something called an interpreter for a hot new microcomputer that had been introduced to the market. Their demonstration went off without a hitch and they were awarded the contract. Having proven that they could work together successfully and come up with an outstanding solution to a complex problem, the two friends formed Microsoft.

It was sometime in the 1980's when our home got its first personal computer. I distinctly remember being a kid and messing around on an IBM computer with the green text and black screen. Yes, people! I have a distinct and clear memory of the IBM/MS-DOS combination which was one of the product collaborations that was instrumental in the tremendous success of Microsoft.

Although this collaboration between Bill and Paul did not last forever, the main ingredients for a collaboration were there at the beginning and those foundations set the company on its path to tremendous and sustained success.

A Sweet Story

One of the points that came up time and again during our *Collaboration Conversations* is that for a collaboration to be truly successful the parties involved must have shared values. Without the same ideals about how to treat customers, how to treat each other, how to treat those we work with, what our do's and don'ts are, where our hard stops are, it is difficult to sustain a partnership or enjoy one that stands the test of time.

I love diving into origin stories of the companies that are a big success. Maybe it is just my lifelong love of learning that kicks in there; but, sometimes I think it may be just the hopefulness of it all. I adore the idea that these people started their businesses on a shoestring and were able to turn that business into what is now a titan of industry. Remarkable! Maybe there is some hopefulness in reading stories like that to remind me that we can succeed with our projects and intentions. This leads me into the sweet, sweet story of Ben and Jerry's, pun absolutely intended.

Did I mention that I love stories like this one? I love how the company started with an ice cream making course that they obtained for only $5. Note also that it was a correspondence course! From a $5 correspondence course on ice cream making has come some of the most delicious ice cream I've ever had (back when I used to do dairy and now they even have non-dairy options - Big Ben and Jerry's free ad here!) I've been to the factory in Vermont, I've done the tour, sat through the movie, tasted as many of the samples as they offered, and then bought more on my way out, plus all the merchandising for my kid! To say I'm a fan of what these dudes started back in 1978 is an understatement. It's no accident that I am sharing my enthusiasm for their business with you.

But it's not all about the deliciousness. The big takeaway for me with Ben and Jerry's is the importance of shared values.

The formal name for the company is Ben and Jerry's Homemade Holdings, Inc. I mean with a name like that you have to just love the company right? Ben and Jerry were buddies since childhood. There was a considered and planned out investment from each partner in the funding of and forming of the company, and both partners were all in. What I think we can learn from most is that the partners had shared values. In 1985 they formed the Ben and Jerry's foundation focused on community projects. Over the years their commitment to charity and social conscience has been legendary, and though they are no longer the principals of this great company, their sweet legacy lives on.

It's the Happiest Collaboration on Earth

There's a reason Disney makes it on my top five list of big businesses that have outstanding collaborations. Certainly there is a lot to be said about the early days of Disney and how that company started but where we can learn, as small businesses, is how Disney partners with EVERYONE. I think of how Disney makes its staff partners part of its cause and how its ubiquitous ability to collaborate with anyone, any brand with similar values, expands its reach and its income and keeps Disney relevant year after year. Disney continues to be one of the most successful companies in the world, especially within the entertainment industry which is arguably one of the more powerful divisions of any economy.

I'm about to age myself, or maybe I won't? Back in the day when I used to be a music aficionado, there was a new young rapper who would consistently make it onto my running playlists. He was little known, maybe a sensation on the mix tape and Spanish reguéton circuit but not too many in the mainstream had heard of him at the time. Then one day everyone knew who Pitbull was. Pitbull partnered with and did duets with other artists like Ke$ha, Christina Aguilera, and Keith Urban to expand into the pop and country market, and with R&B stars who were hot at the time like Chris Brown and Usher. He expanded his reach in the Spanish language market by teaming up with artists like Marc Anthony and Shakira. In the course of doing an abundance of collaborations you will always have the ones that you consider not the best. Is his collaboration with Priyanka Chopra such an example? It's art, there are no objective fails, right?

Nowadays when he refers to himself as "Mr. Worldwide," it's no joke, and if you are breaking out into the pop music arena, hopping onto a collaboration with Pitbull can give you tremendous visibility because he is so well known. You haven't heard of Pitbull? That's OK! I guarantee you have heard his music even if it's just in a commercial. Like Pitbull, Disney collaborates with everyone and their mother.

Disney started out in the 1920's as Disney Brothers Cartoon Studio, a partnership between the brothers, Walter and Roy. One of the things about Walt that I think many of us as entrepreneurs can relate to is that his career had tremendous highs and lows. There were moments when he thought surely this was his time to shine right before his company headed into closure, and, eventually, his vision became a reality and the reality that so many of us enjoy and are touched by every single day.

Looking at the questions that I ask before I enter into a collaboration I can truly say that Disney hit all the marks. Both the Disney brothers were obviously no stranger to each other and had a well thought out partnership at the beginning. Both appeared in alignment and both were focused in their individual areas of expertise. Brother Roy was in the accounting field, and he made sure that he stayed focused on his area of their collaboration. Meanwhile, brother Walt had a huge vision and extreme creativity. Like us over in the small business arena, Disney has had ups and downs over the years but one thing that it continues to do is stay relevant.

Disney does this in a number of ways but one of the ways is through collaborations with just about everyone. You will be able to enjoy a little reminder of your favorite characters or of your visit to the happiest place on earth from the cereals you buy in your local grocery store to your favorite high priced headphones. Disney has collaborations with all kinds of toymakers, jewelers, shoemakers, clothing manufacturers. You name the product, you can probably find a version with a Disney character on it! Disney is not only open to collaborations, it's culture is built on it. That is why so many years later in spite of ups and downs, Disney continues to be a poster child for success in business.

With collaborations like those employed by both Pitbull and Disney, the customer wins. They have an opportunity to enjoy something they consider to be classic and at the same time be introduced to something new and fresh. The newcomer in the collaboration wins by being introduced to new audiences and the established partner in the collaboration gets a refresh to its brand that may be losing relevance. Everyone wins because the combination of the two may bring about a new and novel, perhaps exclusive and unique, product or service that neither collaborator would bring to his audience by working alone.

Fun special mention collabs: Lego and NASA because, well, I love both those things; Harvard and MIT because it's Harvard and MIT, and also because they are considered, in some circles, to be competitors; and, of course, Marvel and Reebok because, I love me my superheroes. If superheroes are out there collaborating then shouldn't we be collaborating also?

Chapter Review

Let's personalize this for you and your business.

1) What was your biggest takeaway from the examples of large companies shared here? What are your favorites?

2) What other big business collaborations come to mind? Are there any that you might like to emulate?

3) What ideas are starting to come to mind for implementation in your business?

Meditation

Take a deep breath for a count of five, hold for a count of seven, and exhale for a count of nine. Repeat five times and feel yourself relax.

Imagine yourself in your business but imagine that you have, over the course of 10 years, formed the most fortuitous collaboration and you are now being interviewed for *Forbes* magazine as an example of what other businesses can learn about a successful collaboration.

1) What does your outstanding example of a business look like?

2) What does it feel like to be at that stage of your entrepreneurial journey?

3) What were the most important things that you did to get to this point?

4) What were the obstacles that you and your partner overcame to stay together and get where you are today?

5) What outstanding words of wisdom do you have for your *Forbes* magazine interviewer?

Grow Smarter

Chapter 5

If It's So Great What's Holding Us Back?

If collaboration is so great, then why isn't everyone doing it? During our limited-edition Ladies' Power Lunch Podcast series, *Collaboration Conversations*, we asked our guests this question. Many answers were what I expected but there were a few unexpected stories that surfaced. We have been able to put the hesitations into nine different categories all centering around fear, mistrust, and a non-collaborative mindset.

From the discussions that I've had with these kind, amazing, powerful, and successful women who often use collaboration as a business growth tool, it seems that the nine main things that hold us back from considering collaboration are:

- Competitive vibe.

- Lack of trust in the other.

- Doubt that the other person is as competent as we might hope.

- Doubt that the other will indeed pull their own

weight.

- The need to control. Wanting to just do everything ourselves. The belief that if I want something done well, I have to do it myself.

- Trust issues might extend to not feeling comfortable letting others behind the scenes of our businesses, just not opening ourselves up to that kind of vulnerability.

- Self-confidence: Trust that I am enough. Thinking that everyone is better than I am.

- Fear of not being listened to and of our decisions not being respected.

- Not being accustomed to collaboration, not being raised in that kind of culture, and not knowing how to proceed.

OK, so let's knock these out one by one. Let's start with the idea of competition. It feels, for me, as though it's closely tied in with not being accustomed to collaboration as a culture, so I'll tie those together.

Most of us were exposed to a world where competition seemed to be the norm. Many kids with siblings have had at least one competitive thought towards their brother or sister in their life, am I right? I mean, for the majority of us, the idea of being the top of our class started as young as kindergarten. All of us can relate to the idea of the proud mom exclaiming to the other equally proud moms that her little Billy had some advantage over their little "Billies" because he had just read the encyclopedia or painted her a Monet! I'm not going to lead you down the Freudian path on this one, but as mothers, is this all our fault?

Fast forward to competitive sports. There was always a winner or a "loo-oo-oo-oo-ser." Who hasn't heard that second place is just the first loser? The degree to which we internalize society's messages of lack will vary from person to person, but the messages are there. They are for many of us part of our programming and so letting go of that and embracing another paradigm can seem counterintuitive.

We all have memories of missing out on something, not getting that Black Friday deal after standing in line for hours, no? That was just me? OK, how about the restaurant running out of the entrée you ordered? If we have all been taught to crush the competition, isn't the competition also going to attempt crushing, and shouldn't we be crushing back? This thought has fed into the idea that scarcity is real and that competition in our business is, at least, a necessary evil or, at its most extreme, a game that we have to win at all costs.

Now, for all you wonderful moms out there on the playground, the truth is all those little angels are amazing. Every. Last. One. They all mature at different rates and they all have different strengths. I believe, on a side note, that we all have some genius. Many of us have never explored the thing that makes us shine, and for some of us the thing that is amazing about us may not be the thing that's particularly embraced, revered, or sought after by society at this time. Like I said, that was just a side note, but it bears out my point that if each of us is focused on our brilliance and on what makes us uniquely us, then there is no chance of someone taking our place. It can't happen.

If we consider the idea of competitive sports, the same reasoning applies. Just because we didn't place first in the sprint doesn't mean we might not be good at the marathon. It just requires a completely different skill set, and your skill set is uniquely suited to you and, guess what, it's also uniquely suited to your ideal client.

How does all this fit into the idea of collaboration? I'd say, do not let the idea of competition keep you from considering collaboration in its many and varied forms. I know members of our LPL community who do the exact same business in the same space and they have each other on speed dial referring business back and forth all day long and everyone flourishes and thrives.

Two women who work in the finance space were

on one of our LPL shows some time ago. They both do pretty much the same thing but both have their preferred client types, and referrals and partnerships happen between them all the time. I had invited one of them to be on the show and she quickly sent me a text asking if the other woman could be on the show as well. Always looking out for each other. Always looking out for each other in a room where there may be opportunities.

One of the reasons that collaborating with someone in your field can be so rewarding is because they may understand your business and its ins and outs better than any other type of business person. Their strengths, the sub-specialty of your field that they like the most, and their special skills in the field may not be the same as yours. The type of client they prefer working with may not be the exact same as you prefer, and their approach to the work may be different. But, this brings new perspectives and new opportunities.

With the right collaboration in this kind of setting it can gain the biggest wins. I think again about how well I worked with partner docs in practice. The patients are always the big winners when we collaborate.

All that being said, at the end of the day it boils down to what you truly believe. Do you believe that you create your own reality, that you attract the right people and circumstances to yourself, and that this world is full and abundant with resources? If you believe that abundance is available for you and that it cannot be taken by another, then you are there.

Trust is trickier and it encompasses a lot:

- Will my collaborator try to pull a fast one, you know, try to cheat us in some way? Take our money? Take our clients?

- Are they competent? Working together puts my reputation at stake. Can they deliver on their promises? Do they know what they are doing? Do they know how to do their piece?

- Are they all in? Will they be reliable, will they give the collaborative project their full effort? Can they afford the time or are they too busy? Will I end up having to pick up the slack?

These are great questions to ask when considering any collaboration. Even though we say innocent until proven guilty, societal dynamics suggest that we may often greet new people, places, and things with some level of mistrust. It's not a bad idea to remain a bit reserved. Survival might, in fact, depend on it. I'm not suggesting you jump into a collaboration with the next person who offers one. I'm suggesting that we not hastily dismiss the idea, as it may be the key to mutual business growth especially during difficult times.

If It's So Great What's Holding Us Back?

You can't ever know everything before going into collaboration, but it's worth it to do your homework. Today, when I should have been writing, I was on the phone with a lovely woman, and as we networked and got to know each other better it became apparent that there was a great opportunity for collaboration. (To be fair, I see collaborations everywhere even in my sleep, sooo...) The problem, or as one of my mentors liked to say "the opportunity for a solution," was that I do not know this woman very well. This may have only been our third conversation, but we liked each other, we knew a lot of the same people, and the energy felt right. So what did I do? I hopped on the texts and reached out to a few people who I know have worked with her in the past. (I hope she did the same for me, too.)

Great news! Of people that I know and trust that have worked with this amazing mystery lady, they all outline her practices as fair. Every single one of them commends her work ethic. One person even commented that she doesn't know when she sleeps. Each and every one of the people I reached out to spoke highly of her treatment of her clients. So, my question is, will she be fair? Is she competent and is she all in? Well, based on the feedback from my trusted sources I would say absolutely. I haven't decided to say yes to the collaboration as yet, in full transparency, but it is definitely on the table and leaning towards a positive conclusion.

The point is I haven't dismissed the idea. I'm always at least open to the idea of a collaboration. If I go down that path it could be very lucrative for both of us, and the clients we both serve would benefit outstandingly! Don't just dismiss the idea of collaboration. You could be leaving money, opportunities, and/or your next big thing on the table! You never know. At least do your homework.

The next step for me in this case will be to have a conversation. We will make sure that we are on the same page and that each party is aware of expectations. For this collaboration, if we decide to go forward, there will also be a simple contract in place, too, to protect everyone's interests.

Let's dive a little deeper into the fear-based reasons for holding back from considering a collaboration.

- Fear of relinquishing control. If I let another take on some tasks will they be done as well as I would do it? What if their approach is different? What effect will that have on the final outcome of the project?

- We all wear some kind of mask as we go through our daily lives. Letting someone into the background of our business can sometimes be scary.

- Fear that we won't be enough or we won't do a

good enough job. Fear that the project may fail and that we may be to blame.

- Fear of not being heard. For those of us coming from a corporate environment, this fear may be even more real and sustaining.

All fear-based premises have the same root. We hold on to our status quo because we believe that if we do not something very bad will happen. But fear tends not to stand up to careful scrutiny, so let's scrutinize away. After we have done our investigation of the suitability of the other person for a partnership, after we have had our conversations, after we have drawn up our contracts, if need be, and are waiting to sign on the line, after we have checked in with our inner knowing, we may still have to grapple with our fears. Or, we could just confront them head on ahead of time!

So, what's the worst that would happen if you relinquish control? The worst is probably that you would end up having to do everything yourself which is probably what you had been planning on anyway? But how likely is that? Have you talked about expectations? Has your research revealed that this person can actually deliver on her promises? If that's the case, then most likely something closer to the best case scenario will occur. There is room here for optimism over fear.

What's the worst that could happen with a stranger behind the scenes? Whatever havoc you might be thinking she could be wreaking is probably a little exaggerated. If there are areas of concern, then limit access. I'll give you an example: I collaborate, refer, and partner with lots of our friends. In my case, however, because of HIPPA regulations I take specific precautions and limit access to certain things. Everyone wins because everyone's privacy is respected. And, I think that mutual respect is going to be a deciding factor in all cases.

When it comes to your personal competence, well, let's be honest. Can you do the thing you are saying you are going to do? Most likely it's a thing that you do for your clients all the time and that you shine at. Often when we feel this fear it is in the shadow of another person that we assume may be at another higher level than us in some way. So hear my words: You are enough. Practice your craft. When you are going into a collaboration give it 100% of your effort. Knowing that you gave it your all will take away the blame even if the project ends up being a bust.

Finally, let's look at the fear of not being heard. If you have ever been the one woman at the conference table, and the youngest one, then this fear is REAL! So the thing about these insidious fears is that they do not come from left field; they are close enough to reality that we accept them as truth. But, if you have a collaboration with a group that does not respect your ideas and does not listen to your input, you would have peeped this early on, way before you get to the point of actually doing something together. When you connect with your collaboration partner, don't only listen to what she is saying, watch how she is behaving. If she isn't listening to your input in the beginning, answering your concerns, communicating effectively in the early stages, then she is not the right partner for you and you should feel free to go back to the collaboration store and ask for a refund. That being said, be sure that it's not just the fear of being steamrolled that's keeping you away from your potentially lucrative collaboration.

Last piece of advice (for now, you know I always have more): This showed up for almost all the women that we interviewed. Leave perfectionism at the door. Even when you are doing a solo project nothing goes 100% as expected. Sometimes things go better, sometimes worse. We have to be open to what comes and be willing to maybe learn the lessons for the next collaboration.

Chapter Review

Let's personalize this for you and your business.

1) You may already be a master collaborator or may just be dipping your toe into that pond. Of the nine key reasons why people hesitate to consider collaborations, do any in particular resonate with you?

2) Are there other reasons not listed that may be holding you back from embracing collaborations? What category do they fall in: competitive vibe, mistrust, or fear?

3) Thinking of your main hesitations, if you were to imagine the worst-case scenario what would that be? What would the best case look like? What measures could you put in place to protect yourself?

Meditation

We are all a product of our environment and our experiences. Everything that makes us up has served us at some time.

Close your eyes and take three deep cleansing breaths. As you sit in your chair, imagine that you can feel the deep connections between you and the earth below. On the next inhale imagine that a bright red light is penetrating your feet from the ground and permeating your entire being from your soles to the top of your head. Imagine that this is a cleansing, purifying energy here to return to the earth, an energy that may have been beneficial for you in the past but which no longer serves you. As you breathe in the energy of the earth, imagine it dissolving away all aberrant feelings of mistrust, fear, competition, not enough-ness, and any other feelings that may be holding you back from living your optimal life. Take a deep breath in and bring your shoulders to your ears while tightening all the muscles that you can in your body. On the exhale, feel all your muscles slowly relax. Breathe in the energy of the earth and breathe out all that no longer serves.

1) What came up for you during this breathing exercise?

2) What feelings are you ready to let go of?

3) Are there any hesitations to let go of any of it? What specifically? How does that inform you?

Chapter 6

How Collaborating Saved My Business, My Sanity, and Maybe My Life

You see people going about their daily lives. People with big smiles on their faces, people who may have tremendous success; we all look at people and make judgments about them. I'd like to say it isn't so but we are creatures of the first impression.

Sandra Yancey, one of the women that I consider to be a great mentor, likes to remind us that success and failure are on the same road and that success is just a bit farther along. Napoleon Hill mentions miners who had no success for a good long time until they hit the vein that produced everything they were looking for. If you look at every motivational book, if you listen to any motivational speaker, they talk about the path to success being less than direct.

I was just talking to one of my patients in my practice. Turns out that the thing he was coming in for was a bit similar to what I experienced while doing my up-dogs in my yoga practice that morning. We jokingly came to the conclusion that perhaps the reason that I go through times that one could consider less than ideal is for the purpose of helping those I come into contact with to better understand their challenge and, in so doing, overcome it. Who knows? Maybe? If me coming out of the closet about my financial struggles in my businesses helps another then it was worth sharing.

What I have to share here is the story of how collaboration saved my business, saved my sanity, and maybe it's not a stretch to say it saved my life? You decide. Maybe in sharing this story, we will be encouraged to look beyond the surface, to be kinder to each and every soul that we encounter, to suspend judgment, and, oh yes, to be open to how collaboration can be a tactical tool for scaling our businesses.

We have all seen that meme on social media which shows what people think the path to success looks like and the twists and turns, ups and downs that it entails in reality. We have also heard time and again "don't judge a book by its cover" and platitudes of this nature probably from the moment we have been able to mentally process platitudes. So, you will not be surprised that my story had some twists, and you will also agree that, just like every one of us, I continue evolving.

Some of you may have heard a portion of this story before. Usually I share it in the context of what was going on with my health at the time, but this time around I'm going to share some stuff that is coming from a more vulnerable place. The truth is, I have hardly any hesitation sharing with others that I had a health issue. Maybe it's my own personal way of thinking about things, but I don't judge myself harshly about it, and if my health journey helps another, I'm happy to share it. But sharing about challenges in my business? For those of you who have met me, who have heard me speak, or have read what I write, you will probably recognize that I have not shared my struggle in this area. Until now.

I'll give the short notes version of what was going on with my health. I'd had my baby, and for the first 18 months he would not sleep through the night so, obviously, neither did I. In an effort to lose the baby weight, I signed up for and started training for the Hartford Marathon. After working all day, training for a marathon, and taking care of my baby all night, well, my body started cracking under the pressure to say the least. Six physicians and two unnecessary surgeries later, I was in the office one afternoon smiling at patients through the pain as I hobbled on crutches, trying to help everyone else's pain (I know, the irony is not lost on me) when the voice of God through one of my patients said, "Doc, you have to go take care of yourself." It was my doctor-heal-thyself moment.

For the first time in the history of the known

universe I closed our office and got in to see a specialist almost immediately on an emergency basis. I've worked in teaching hospitals and teaching clinics over my almost 20 years in health care, and I know that when your specialist calls in the other docs and the students, well, let's just say your condition is a tad serious. Someone said after I had been poked and prodded, "It must be autoimmune." Finally I was able to take my blinders off and see what was going on with me. At that point I knew exactly what I needed to do. It was super simple! I would treat myself exactly the same way I would treat my patients, using holistic, nutrition-based solutions. This story has a happy ending, and within six months I was well on the way to my recovery.

So, here's the bit I never get into, the part about how my business was doing during this time. I went back to work six short weeks after the birth of my baby. I was new to our practice and I needed to build a bit of a following. Many of us who go to professional schools know a whole lot about treating our patients, or whatever the content of our profession is, when we leave school but know little to nothing of growing a practice, managing a practice, and making money in a business. I was one of those. We think we are just going to hang our shingle and that patients will find us, but it's not that simple. My timing was not great. I bought into my practice in the middle of an economic downturn. What that meant is that our patient base was not doing well financially. Many had lost their jobs and their health insurance and, suddenly, routine care visits became a hardship for them. To pile on, after the government shut down, we lost our Medicaid credential. That was an entire portion of our patient population that we were no longer able to treat.

I was fortunate to get some good advice from mentors to join the local Chamber of Commerce that led to me attending, literally, I am not exaggerating, y'all, thousands of networking events. I made a lot of connections and got to know a lot of amazing people in our area, and maybe my practice did grow a bit, but certainly nowhere near where it needed to be. I had practice bills piling up and then, as luck would have it, we had not one, but two, floods in our office. The insurance payouts were less than we expected, and did not cover all the necessary repairs and replacements from the damage. Between property insurance deductibles and reducing reimbursements from the health insurance companies, I was truly stumped. I needed more patients.

I had done all the things that were recommended. I was religiously getting to early morning networking meetings and attending all the "business-after-hours" that I could find. If there was an opportunity to speak somewhere about health and wellness, I volunteered. If there was a health fair (usually on the weekends), I was there, plus I was keeping early and late hours in my practice to accommodate the patients that we did have at the time. I was doing coffee dates with anyone who would invite it from all my networking, but all that seemed to happen, from my perspective, was that people would come to coffee or lunch, talk at me about their business, exhibit very little interest in my practice, and then ask me to buy their widget. Have you ever experienced that? What you thought was intended to be a mutual exchange of ideas turns into a one-way street?

I was on social media. I had a blog, I wrote articles for the local paper, I did print advertising, I reached out to the other local physicians for referrals. Trust me. I was doing all the things. I got a business coach and I learned to do all the things well. All this with a small child and the above mentioned health issues. I'm going to get truly naked here, and I don't even understand my hesitation to share this little tidbit, but I have even had to defer my student loans to pay my staff. I just was not getting the return on the time and money investment that I was putting in.

I remember it as if it were yesterday. It was a Monday. It was the third Monday in the month to be exact. I have always been a connector. Back in high school and in college, back when dinosaurs roamed the earth, I always ended up with friends from varied backgrounds. Thinking back, I realize that I was always able to bring them together with little or no effort. That day, without even thinking about it, just doing what came naturally for me, I invited five of the women that I had met at various networking things to come have lunch together with me. One was an HR manager at a not-for-profit, one was a videographer, one woman sold greeting cards, one was a banking vice president, and one was a real estate agent. I tell you their professions because I want to emphasize that they were not necessarily in allied fields. We could network with each other maybe, but the ways that we could form joint venture partnerships wasn't just leaping out at us.

What is interesting is these women and I had one thing in common. We were all focused on growing; whether it was a practice, a client base, the position in a corporate career; we were all driven, focused women, and like recognizes like. We all sat down to lunch. This may have been one of the best hours plus that I have ever spent. We talked about our jobs, we talked about our lives. What was interesting is that even though we were all in different fields, we all understood each other's frustrations, we all rejoiced in each other's triumphs, we all could relate to, or even give advice for another's problem or concern. By the time we left that lunch we were fast friends. To this day, if I'm on the side of a road and need help these are some of the women that I know I can call on because their concern is real, and they always know they can call on me.

That day at that table when someone had a concern we were able to mastermind to a solution. Connections, referrals, and collaborations were happening left and right. People were pulling out their phones and making connections on the spot. There was an intentionality about it that had been missing from every single networking event that I had ever attended, even the ones that said they were focused on the giving part. It was my first experience with this sort of thing. I had stumbled upon it completely by accident, and I craved more. So did my friends. Amidst comments that we should really do this more often, ever the practical one, I realized that unless someone did something in that moment, a second meeting would, literally, never happen. It had taken so much time and effort to arrange this date, to get everyone's calendars to agree as it was, and, so, I suggested my idea.

"Here's what we'll do, we will put it on the calendar. We will meet once per month. Let's make it the third Monday of the month at 12:30 pm."

And, so, dear one, in the dining room of a Ruby Tuesday on Route 6 in Bristol, Connecticut, the idea of what has now grown into Ladies' Power Lunch (LPL) was born. LPL has become more of a movement than anything else. It's a growing space for women in business to connect with each other for free and we only have one rule: WE INTENTIONALLY SUPPORT EACH OTHER!

How Collaborating Saved My Business, My Sanity & Maybe My Life

Yes, I know what you are thinking, 'So you had a delicious and healthy lunch, made some new friends! Good for you! But how did that save your sanity, your business, and, arguably, your life? Sounds like a stretch to be honest.' You aren't wrong; it sounds like a stretch but what happened next is what iced the cake on this, and it is the power of collaboration at work.

Collaboration has many different levels. It can range from its simplest form of a referral partnership to a more advanced business partnership. Among those five women at that table that day, and in the months that followed, intentional collaborations took place. These five women were perfectly aligned for this. As I mentioned before, I had been networking my behind off for a while, so you can imagine that my list of connections and potential referrals was very long. Every opportunity that I had to point business in their direction, they were front of mind for me, and wouldn't you know it, for the first time in a long time it was reciprocated.

Right place, right time, right women! I mentioned the careers of these women because I want you to understand that there was no obvious collaboration potential there, but there was intention, and, to this day, I am forever enriched for having these amazing souls as part of my journey. As a result of supporting the woman who sells greeting cards, I had a tremendous mindset shift. She taught me to remember the power of gratitude.

We started truly appreciating and loving up our existing patient base. We would usually send holiday and birthday cards, but we extended our card-giving spree to include, "Thanks for joining our practice," "Great to see you," and "Awesome that you are feeling better," just to name a few. These were all sentiments that were heartfelt, but actually sending patients a card saying this stuff reminded me that we were blessed to have the patients that we did have. Patients loved it! They started sending us cards, too, bringing us little tokens of appreciation. It deepened our relationship with our patient base creating more of a family feeling, and, suddenly, we started seeing patients referring their husbands, wives, grandparents, neighbors, coworkers, and bringing in their children. All from the power of sending a little card to express a sentiment that I was already feeling.

Even in this day and age of technology, we still, years later, continue to send out a lot of the same campaigns that we did back then. I've also been able to give heart-felt testimonials for appreciation marketing at every turn and continue to recommend appreciation marketing to every business person that I come across looking for a way to grow her business. Something as simple as a card can change things in a big way.

One of the women at lunch with us is a

videographer, she and I had babies that were similar ages, and, so, over play dates and birthday parties we planned our networking strategies. She became my networking partner. I'd call her and tell her of upcoming events and she would do the same. If you have ever walked into a networking event packed with people you do not know it can be daunting, but we had each other. We strode into these events with confidence, and, trust me when I tell you, being comfortable, confident, and at ease does a lot for your delivery. Just saying; people are more likely to trust a doctor that looks confident and not nervous, am I right?

Such a gift! I remember back then introducing her to marketers and website developers who were a perfect fit for what she is doing. She is amazingly talented and is still my go to person for all things video. If anyone needs a videographer she's the one I reach out to. She is in the marketing world and so with her help, we upgraded my practice's website, adding video. She even encouraged me to start capturing video testimonials from patients that wanted to do them: with my iPhone! This was years ago before this was the norm, but she was and still is on the cutting edge. She helped me become comfortable on video; also, looking at me now, making five YouTube videos a week, we realize she has created a monster!

I mentioned that one of my FAB FIVE is in the

not-for-profit sector. Over the years she has become an amazing friend. We have worked so well together on a number of projects. We have, on many occasions, brainstormed ways that we could possibly go into a true business partnership. It hasn't happened as of yet but, watch out world, when we do, it will be phenomenal. I envision someday starting the Ladies' Power Lunch Foundation, and I can think of exactly who I'd love to have run it!

You don't work in a nonprofit and not make lots of connections. My list of contacts was deep, but she had me beat! Through her influence, I ended up being appointed to different boards, being invited to speak at various events, and becoming the go to physician for a particular sporting endeavor. This was an amazing partnership. We worked side by side on a project to increase awareness of her organization. I was having so much fun supporting and giving back that I didn't even realize that it was raising my profile in our community. Suddenly local papers wanted to interview me, more speaking things were coming my way, and did I mention I was having a ton of fun? As for that not-for-profit: even today, that is one of the ones that we support with the Ladies' Power Lunch Fund which is our give back.

Moving from a competitive mindset, which I didn't even know I was in, to a collaborative mindset may have been the biggest boon of all. I can truly credit one of the women who shared lunch with us on that very first LPL day for a lot of the mindset shifts that I have had. I think that may have been the first and biggest step to transforming my business trajectory. I needed to change my mind, and I did. I was no stranger to the self-help and personal development space. One of my mentors likes to joke that she spent 10 years in the self-help aisle, and I usually respond, "I've got you beat sister, by about a decade!" There is a difference, though, between knowing something intellectually, and actually embodying it.

I knew that competition was a mental construct, yet deep down inside I worried. I'd used traditional marketing templates and, so, most of my marketing was focused on "crushing the competition." But, the next member of my fab five changed everything. We bonded over our love of personal development but she was a bit farther along than I was and, frankly, some of the stuff that she was reading was a little bit too woo woo even for me back then. But bond we did. I remember her encouraging words when I confided in her about my student loan situation. She told me her story and assured me that someday I'd have significant operating income. She mentioned a figure that to me seemed so far off, and now to be able to look at my business operating account and to see that it is about double that figure fills me with gratitude.

She and I swapped books, well, to be quite

honest, it was mostly her giving me books to read and making amazing recommendations. We went to self-help seminars together, and experienced all kinds of miracles. I remember coming up with a business idea right after we had attended a personal development event. That business venture is still a part of our practice even today. In the bright shining light of her friendship, I grew my personal development and spirituality and have been able to embrace all the parts of me, even my incredible intuition. I learned to trust the universe and not look to the circumstances to define my emotions. I teach this today. The spark was always there but in her presence it grew to a roaring flame. To this day, like clockwork, if I'm down or having a meh day, miraculously a text shows up in my inbox with an inspirational thought or video or something from her. She is always on time.

And yes, yes, we did have an amazing referral relationship. One of the cornerstones of collaboration is trust. I remember her referring her mother-in-law to our practice. Now that's trust! The trust was, and continues to be, absolutely mutual. This was someone that I could trust to be there for someone I sent to her. I never have any hesitation.

Let me tell you a quick story. I had a patient who was in pain. This man, even though he was older, should not have been in as much pain as he was, and still nothing seemed to be working. Finally, one day I sat down with him in the office and I asked him what was going on. He explained. He had been carrying two mortgages for about a year. His old house could not sell and he was living in his new home. The financial burden was near killing him. I told him to wait right there. I got on the phone with my friend. She's a high-powered busy realtor but she took my call immediately, and before long she got his property listed and under contract. All within a month, and also all while she was significantly pregnant. I remember this specifically because her baby was born on Christmas, and the property closed right after the New Year. As for my patient, he was so relieved, his huge stressor was removed, and his pain improved almost miraculously. Then he started spreading the word among his friends that I was a miracle worker.

The collaborations ran the gamut. I smile as I think about one woman sending me her husband as a patient and him saying to me: "I'm only here because my wife sent me. I hate doctors." That was the beginning of a beautiful friendship!

They are all the best, and I save the most collaboration-based story for last. I ended up forming an unlikely business partnership with one of the women. Turns out that her corporate career was great but her true passion was health and wellness. This is not something I would ever have known from casual networking at an after-hours event. She and I continue to have a robust financially linked business partnership to this day.

And, as for my business and prospects? Well, you've probably guessed it: our practice was able to see growth in spite of the economic downturn and natural disasters. Our growth allowed us to take on staff, open a satellite office location (thanks to my business bestie), and add services and equipment.

It has been my experience in practice that people find it most difficult to maintain a stress-free demeanor when they have issues with their health, relationships, or their finances. During that time in my life, stress relating to finances was surely affecting my health as well as my mental and emotional well-being. Learning how to remain low stress in spite of the circumstances was an invaluable lesson that came out of this time, and this is why I can now teach with such strong conviction that happiness does not depend on circumstances, and that we will always get by with a little help from our friends.

Chapter Review

Let's personalize this for you and your business.

1) Have you ever had a financially stressful time in your business? What comes to mind?

2) What were your biggest challenges?

3) Looking back, is there any way that your situation could have been improved by employing the power of the collective, using the idea of intentional collaboration?

4) Considering your next year in business: What financial concerns come to mind for you? What are your biggest challenges?

5) Considering the idea of intentional mutual support, outline an idea for a collaboration that could support your business.

6) What is your hesitation when it comes to collaboration?

7) What would have to be in place for this hesitation to no longer be a factor for you?

8) As far as collaborations in your business go, what would you want to get out of it?

9) What would you be willing to contribute?

10) What sort of business could be an ideal collaborator for you?

11) Where would you find such a collaboration partner?

12) How can you go about taking the first steps to making that connection a reality?

Meditation

Close your eyes. Take three deep breaths and imagine that you are floating in the void. Around you is clear and white; it is calm and peaceful surrounded by pure nothingness. Take a few moments to breathe into the peace and tranquility of this void, and then notice that a menu pops up giving you the opportunity to fill the void in any way that you like. You have the opportunity to select the people, experiences, and things that fill this beautiful void. Imagine as you look at this endless menu of choices that you are holding an easy button and that you are able to just pick and choose the items that please you the most.

1) If you had no limitations and you really allowed yourself to dream, what would your business look like within the next year?

2) What sort of supportWhat would be optimal for you in this ideal vision of your business?

3) What sort of clients or customers can you envision?

4) What does your downtime look like, how are you spending your time away from your business?

5) How much time do you want to spend in your business?

6) What collaboration partnerships do you see in your future?

Part II

Five Steps to Abundance through Collaboration

I've picked a lot up along my trail and as Oprah says, there are a lot of things that I can say that I know for sure. I can say that for every collaboration that I have done, which now number into the thousands, If I went through these five pillars, things went swimmingly and peachy keen. If I skipped a step or skipped my process in its entirety, then there was no guarantee of success. Sometimes in going through my process I'd be able to arrive at things that would make the collaboration better, get improved ideas, or sometimes I'd realize the collaboration was not for me, possibly a great idea for another person, or for another time. I've mentioned parts of my process before but let's list them all here.

The five pillars that help me succeed in collaboration are:

1) **Ask:** Contemplation, Clarity, and Spaciousness

2) **Alignment:** Energy, Communication, Trust, and Openness

3) **All In:** Commitment, Cooperation and Detachment

4) **Assignment:** Brilliance, Genius, and Special Talents

5) **Applications and Resources:** Technology, Delegation, and Support

In Part II, we'll go into collaborations in more detail, bringing in more of the amazing wisdom that I gleaned from interviewing our LPL members on our limited series, *Collaboration Conversations.*

Chapter 7

Ask

Growing up I always had a deep sense of knowing. As a child you think nothing of it. It just is. But as you start to truly understand the world around you and rely on those around you to smooth your path and ease your way, you may take on their ideas of life. Sometimes this may lead you to let go of what you know to be your truth.

As a young child, I had a very accurate sense of knowing. It would almost seem to an outside observer that it was somewhat magical. Now, looking back, I realize there was no "magic" per se, there was just tuning in to my intuition. I remember very clearly asking my mom to step back. I was very insistent about it. She did step back and very shortly after a window broke. If she had been standing where she was before, shards of glass may have injured her. This sounds way more dramatic than it was and there was no magic involved.

I think back to the feeling I had in the moment and it was clear and sure, sort of like a gut feeling. There was no "message from beyond" telling me the window would break or anything like that. It was just a deep knowing that standing where we had been standing, was not a good idea. At that age and stage of life, I was new and hadn't as yet learned not to trust my instincts and so I pulled on my mommy's hand and pulled her back as a few seconds later the glass shattered.

How many people have had experiences like that? Experiences as a child or as an adult where you either followed your "gut feeling" and things went exactly as you expected. Or, how many times have we not listened to our little voice inside and then regretted our decision in a huge way some time later?

I will never be arrogant enough to pretend to have all the answers to exactly how the universe works. There is a lot I don't know and do not understand. If we had this conversation years ago I would probably have had a perspective that is a little different, but as I live more life and come to greater understanding, I can truly say that there is value to listening to our guidance, however that guidance shows up for us.

For me, my guidance shows up as an inner dialogue that is difficult to explain to others. I've talked to many people who share that their guidance comes more in the way of a feeling, sort of like their body is speaking to them. Some have explained their intuition as an immediate knowing or idea that pops to mind, while I've had others who have expressed that their knowing comes more over time. I've had a lot of people who say that they "always have to sleep on it."

How does your guidance show up? Are you an in the moment decision maker? Do you need to "sleep on it? Do you need more time? Here are some more questions for you: Do you have evidence in your life of how your intuition works? Have you seen how things turn out when you do listen to it? How trusting are you of your inner knowing? What would be available to you if you were able to be even more trusting of yourself?

Now that we are thinking deeply about our intuition, inner knowing, guidance, whatever you call it, you are probably thinking, 'OK, Dr. Davia, this is great. Truly an opportunity for introspection, but what on earth does this have to do with growing our businesses smarter and letting go of stress and strain? How will this increase our incomes so we can live our optimal lives and increase our impact? How will it help us fulfil our dreams of reaching the people we are sent to reach with our messages that are so important? What does the one thing have to do with the other?

The answer is in pillar one of the Grow Smarter paradigm: ASK.

It's not what you think. I'm absolutely not sending

you out at this first stage in the collaboration process to ask anyone to collaborate with you. Rather, I am inviting you to spend some time asking yourself, getting to know what it is that YOU want from a collaboration and what your thoughts and ideas are. First we know ourselves, then we can know the others!

This is an opportunity to spend time in quiet contemplation. How often do we truly allow ourselves to dream? Dream as big as we would like to. Envision what it would be like to have our optimal business. Take time to think about what would happen if there were no barriers and we were building from scratch. What would it look like? Who would our clients be? How many would we be seeing? What kind of support would we have? What kind of collaborations would be ideal for nurturing the kind of dream you are dreaming? Spending time dreaming may sound like a counterintuitive idea but as Darla LeDoux taught me, if you can dream it, if you can see it visualize it and embody it, then the way to make it into a reality that you can take in with your actual senses of touch, taste, smell, hearing and seeing, is possible.

Science shows that visualization does work. It is well known and demonstrated in controlled trials that when we visualize an action, we stimulate the same pathways in the brain that we would if we actually physically performed the action. These principles are actually used in medicine for treating patients with certain kinds of brain damage. It's that powerful. We have all heard of how well visualization, the simple act of intentional and aligned "daydreaming," has been the fuel for some of our most famous athletes achieving feats that seem to defy gravity.

What if we took this powerful tool of contemplation: Asking the source of all that is, what our ideal business could look like, and then being quiet, giving ourselves some spaciousness, and letting our answers unfold. What if we took this tool used by physicians and athletes and applied it to our business? What amazing results would we be able to achieve? How close could we get to defying the "laws" that seem to hold us back, keep us stagnant and small?

Giving ourselves time and space to go within can allow us to achieve clarity that might not have been possible otherwise. Moving forward from this place using our #1 collaboration partner can bring us results that surprise and delight.

Spend Some Time in Contemplation

Speaking on our LPL limited series: *Collaboration Conversations*, Tonia Tyler, YouTube and visual media coach and creative mentions the value of knowing one's self, what you want from your business, and what you would desire from a collaboration. Being clear and not just rushing into things seems to be a theme that came up time and again during our *LPL Collaboration Conversations* interviews. Seeking clarity before all else is the recommended first step to a successful collaboration. Being clear on what we want is also important in optimal communication. Once we are clear on what our goals, dreams, and boundaries are, then we are in a position to know what will be absolutely important to communicate with our partner/collaborator. Without that knowledge, communication is halted in its tracks.

Tonia shares the story about her collaboration with a particular virtual assistant on a specific project. Tonia may have required a certain outcome, but she notes that she was not clear in her mind at the start of the project as to what kind of skill set her collaboration partner needed to bring to the table. After getting deep into the project she realized that her outcome needs were not being met.

Tonia is very adamant that the problem was not that her virtual assistant was incapable, it was that she, Tonia, did not spend the requisite time at the beginning of the project getting clear about the areas she hoped to be supported on. She was able to recognize that the problem was not with her collaboration partner, but with her lack of clarity. She was able to go within, give herself some spaciousness and employ contemplation. Only then was she able to find a new more appropriate partner for that specific collaboration. Further, she notes that her initial partner is better suited for a collaboration that requires a different skill set, and that they may get together again in the future.

Chapter Review

Let's personalize this for you and your business.

1) How tuned in are you to your intuition?

2) What activities do you find help you to be attuned?

    a) Meditation?

    b) Exercise?

    c) Journaling?

    d) Reading/listening to inspirational content?

3) Whatever activity helps you to be attuned, what would happen if you engaged in this activity consistently, even for a short period, daily over the next 21 days?

Meditation

Take a deep breath for a count of four, hold for a count of four, and exhale for a count of four. Repeat for three times and feel yourself relax.

Ask yourself the questions:

1) Am I ready for a collaboration?

2) What kind of collaboration would be optimal for me at this time?

3) What do I have to bring to a collaboration?

4) What complementary skills would my optimal collaboration partner have?

5) What are my values that are non-negotiable where a collaboration is concerned?

6) What is my next step?

Take a few minutes to engage in quiet mind meditation. If you are an avid quiet mind meditator then set a timer for 15-20 minutes. If quiet mind meditation is new to you, then set your timer for seven minutes.

Focus on your breath. Breathe in for a count of four, hold for a count of four, exhale for a count of four. Imagine you are looking at a clear cloudless sky; there is nothing else in your field of vision except for blue clear sky.

Thoughts may intrude, and if they do, imagine they are clouds floating away out of your field of vision, and again focus on your breathing while imagining the beautiful cloudless sky.

Once your timer is done, and when it feels right, take out your journal and make notes, *revisiting* the same questions:

1) Am I ready for a collaboration?

2) What kind of collaboration would be optimal for me at this time?

3) What do I have to bring to a collaboration?

4) What complementary skills would my optimal collaboration partner have?

5) What are my values that are non negotiable where a collaboration is concerned?

6) What is my next step?

7) What came up for you? What new insights were revealed?

Chapter 8

Alignment

When I lean into the idea of a collaboration, once I have asked, my next step is to check in with my alignment. Often this is a solitary activity, however, if there is a potential collaboration partner, then I check in or investigate, if you will, our alignment with each other.

I tend to spend some time in quiet contemplation in order to determine what my inner knowing is saying about this opportunity. Many of us don't trust our inner knowing or intuition nearly enough. I've been guilty of ignoring it on so many occasions, and now I'm doing a better job of inviting my intuition into the discussion.

I also ask myself questions concerning trust: Do I trust the other person? Am I trusting the universe and trusting that what comes to me is either what I am energetically available for or what is energetically lined up with me.

I also ask myself if I am, in fact, open to what is available. Am I maintaining my energy levels so that I can attract high energy collaborations? I ask myself, am I open to what is possible? Sometimes we think things are going to go a specific way but the universe, who I think has a tremendous sense of humor, sometimes has other plans that surprise and delight. Am I open to things unfolding as they will? Am I bringing no judgment to the process or the outcome?

Finally, am I open to learning? Sometimes the things that seem to be negative, or situations that go in unexpected ways are the ones that prepare us for coming attractions or they are the ones that teach us our greatest lessons. Asking myself if I am, indeed, open to the learning reminds me to have no attachment and no judgment regarding outcomes.

What is My Inner Knowing Saying?

I had an outstanding conversation with oracle, model, and authenticity coach, Robin Finney. Robin says that her biggest focus when going into a collaboration is alignment. She admits to having a strong gut sense. And, for an oracle, we would expect that. But I think this applies to every single one of us. Hearing her go on about her gut sense makes me smile because who of us has not had that situation where we felt our gut telling us something, denied our inner knowing, and was sorry after? We can all relate to that, for sure.

Robin tells the story of a woman who she was collaborating with on a photo shoot. She mentions having a gut feeling that, "No, this is not going to work." She went ahead with it anyway, making all sorts of plans. She basically taught her collaborator the entirety of the how-to's of her process. In the end, her partner dropped out of their collaboration and went on to do a similar project solo, using the information she had learned from Robin.

Look, I want to make sure you are taking the right lesson away from this. Yes, it's true this woman was not necessarily the best collaboration partner, but the thing we don't want to miss here is that *Robin had already said "no" to this project.* Her intuition, inner guidance, gut feeling, whatever you want to call it, had, in effect, warned her away from this collaboration, and she pushed through anyway without doing additional due diligence. Great lesson from what, on its surface, appears to be a bad experience.

Since then, Robin says she has gone on to create amazing retreats and other offerings in conjunction with other partners. She has been more careful about communicating goals and aspirations ahead of time and has been quick to speak up. She has remained focused on working in her brilliance and making her partnerships a win-win, and, most importantly, she has respected the role that her intuition plays in helping her to choose her collaboration partners. She notes that her intuition is not the only factor, but that it is definitely an important piece of the puzzle.

One last juicy tidbit that came out of my conversation with Robin is that sometimes when our intuition gives us pause it's not that the collaboration is never intended to happen. Sometimes it could be a matter of timing. It could be that the collaboration is not meant to happen right now.

I asked Mary Ann Pack about knowing when a collaboration is in alignment. I figured that this would be a good question for her since she is a transformation coach and intuitive guide. Her response was spot on. She says that even when a collaboration may look good on paper always ask yourself the question, "Does this endeavor bring me JOY?" She notes that both she and the participants on her podcast have to come to a decision as to whether they move forward with recording.

She instructs us to feel for that *spark of excitement or joy* or the intuitive hit that this is right. She says, "*It has to feel good, it has to resonate with your soul.*" If you are feeling none of this then it is either that the timing is wrong, and it might be an idea that still has time to gestate. She goes on to note that it may also be an idea for someone else, and you may have the opportunity and joy of connecting two meant-to-be collaborators to each other.

Do I Trust the Other Person?

Special LPL Collaboration Conversations guest,

Alignment

Tina Forsythe, a business coach, says that the biggest mistake that people make when hopping into a collaboration is hopping in too quickly and not listening to the gut. Some time ago this very thing happened to Tina. She was in a down season in her business, and someone came along and they started doing a few projects together.

She says that the way she was feeling at the time around her business was not, in retrospect, the most positive. She emphasized that, logically, she was thinking that it would be good to have someone with whom to collaborate, but the gut part of her kept telling her, "Something is not right here." In this case it wasn't a horror story, but it was more of a mismatch. Logically and on paper this collaboration should have worked, and she spent months struggling to make it work with no success. She reminds us to learn from her experience and to, "Listen to our gut and our intuition."

Similar to our other guests, Tina reminds us that it may be that it is not a right fit and sometimes it may just be a case of bad timing. She also reminds us, "Don't be afraid to have the tough conversations. Know up front who is responsible for what tasks, what is the revenue split, and an important piece - who is responsible for marketing and what exactly is each person's responsibility in that regard."

Doing worse case scenario planning at the

beginning can save a relationship when a program or project does not go as planned. If you don't do this kind of planning in the beginning, it can end up in a blame game. She concludes that it is better to talk too much than to leave something unsaid.

Am I Trusting the Universe?

Being able to bounce ideas off each other and having ideas flow is one reason that one of my interviewees, Dena Otrin, likes collaborations. Dena is a licensed professional counselor and she has been in the field of mental health for 21 years. Her advice: Be open to what the universe wants to send you.

She gives the example of recently setting the intention of being open to what the universe wanted to send her. Within days she was invited by another LPL member to collaborate on an unusual and exciting event - one that she might not have considered if left to her own devices. She was invited by her collaborator, who runs a boutique, to host a book signing at her store. The boutique provided the venue, hosted a fashion show with the store's fashions, and Dena had a book reading and signing. The result was an unusual and very engaging event that everyone benefited from! Both collaborators were able to grow their businesses, and the clients benefited from having an outstanding evening of entertainment and education.

Alignment

Dena encourages us to be courageous in recognizing a collaboration, approaching potential collaborators, and in talking about the hard questions at the beginning.

Am I Open to What is Available?

Chatting with Nadine Mullings, a marketing coach, on our LPL *Collaboration Conversations* was effortless. As effortless, perhaps, as the collaborations that she mentions in the stories that she shared with us. Nadine is always open to collaboration and open to what is available. She defines collaboration as co-creation to develop a bigger vision that benefits others. She notes that the final product of a collaboration is greater than or better than what each participant would be able to produce on her own. She also notes that when we come together the collective creative energy is elevated. I adore that definition.

I asked Nadine to give us a few examples of how being open to what is available served to increase her impact and income, and she tells the story of moving to Atlanta. She says she spent the first two years there networking and getting to know the people in the area and she happened upon a woman with whom her personality flowed really well. They were able to co-create a women's conference not just once but two years in a row. What stood out for her with this collaboration is that the coming together was effortless. Yes, putting together an event is a lot of work, but none of the effort was spent working out personality issues. Both members of this collaboration complemented each other, they encouraged each other, they had complementary skill sets, and their visions and goals were in alignment.

Nadine tells another story about coming together to collaborate with a group of nine other women to create a gratitude journal. The project resonated with her, she found it joyful, and as she spoke to me about the project I could literally see her face light up! She notes that one of the things that made the gratitude journal such a success was being open to and seeing what was available.

Collaborating with nine other women was a tremendous increase in her visibility. Suddenly she was reaching a much larger audience than she would have were she working on this alone. Something else that she mentioned, that to be honest I never gave much thought to, is that doing collaborations increased her skill set. Interestingly, she learned leadership and coordination skills during her collaboration. She was then able to take these skills to her business and make that bigger and better.

Collaborations are a staple for Nadine, however, she admits that she mainly thought about collaborations for books and events. That changed forever, and now she is more open to what is available than ever before, as a result of a collaboration that she had with another marketer to offer a 5-day challenge to clients. She mentions that each person was working in her area of brilliance. She showed the clients how to use their blogs to make more of an impact and revenue. Her collaboration partner looked at how clients use their websites for income generation. This sounds like a great challenge, by the way, and it is no wonder that the coming together of these two minds resulted in increased value to the customers.

We always learn from the ones that don't go as well as we might have hoped, and though Nadine jokingly says that all her collaborations go well, she does admit that there is one project that she has been working on for the last two years that has not been as effortless as collaborations usually are for her. This collaboration has suffered from conflicts of personalities, conflicts of other types, delays, slowness, and just overall difficulties.

Nadine's advice for avoiding collaborations that are not ideal:

- Ahead of the process, go through everything.

- Have a signed agreement.

- Make sure it is a document that everyone agrees to.

- Make sure that the lead person on the project is someone you trust.

Am I Open to What is Possible?

One woman in our LPL group with whom I have personally collaborated with is Carol Tsacoyeanes, a personal stylist and sales director with a direct sales company called Ruby Ribbon. It's unlikely that a physician and a purveyor of women's undergarments would collaborate, but we have done so very successfully, as she carries a line of products that promote women's breast health. Who would have "thunk" it!

An outstanding nugget that came out of our conversation on LPL *Collaboration Conversations* was that we have to be really discerning and be in tune with ourselves so that we do not mistake not feeling energy in the moment to complete a task with the complete absence of a positive energetic connection. Carol tells an outstanding story of a collaboration that did a lot to increase her impact and income, and this story bears out this point perfectly.

Carol had a wonderful energetic connection with a client who is a professional ballroom dancer. The client uses Carol's contouring undergarments under her beautiful competition clothing to enhance her silhouette. One day this client, that Carol had such a beautiful energetic connection with, invited her to attend one of her ballroom dancing competitions. It was out of state and at least an hour and a half away.

The idea of driving that far, perhaps when she was already feeling a little tired and low energy, may have stopped her from taking her client up on this opportunity. However, Carol was tuned in to the energetic connection that she had with this customer. The energetic connection was so electric and positive that in spite of her physical energy waning she said, "Yes." Carol took a few samples of the undergarments that she sells just on the off chance that someone might be interested, and wouldn't you know, people asked!

It turned out that this was a regional competition, spanning several states. Multiple vendors who were on site selling their beautiful ballroom dancing competition wear were interested in being able to source the unique undergarments that Carol sells as they would enhance the beauty of their creations. This allowed Carol to expand her reach into a new market and into new states in a truly meaningful and impactful way, all because she was open to what was possible and was able to differentiate between her flagging physical energy and the electric energy of connection.

Carol advises us to be willing and open to possibility, to approach collaborations as a two-way street, to not be the one who is unable to follow through or goes missing. She encourages us to be open-minded, to ask ourselves where our avatars are "shopping," and to explore the idea of collaborations with people who are connected to our ideal clients. And last but not least, Carol emphasizes the importance of planning ahead carefully and being on the same page with your collaboration partner. She says, "Create the vision of the collaboration you want first."

Am I Open to Learning?

Our conversation with Tabatha Waters, a founding member of the organization National Coaching Professionals, brought out that collaborations are outstanding because they offer the opportunity to grow an idea. There is a greater chance of success when bringing together the talents of more than one as compared to what is available to us when we are working alone. Tabatha's words of wisdom are, "When you are in a group and birth an idea together, the idea is as much yours as it is mine because what comes out is a product of all the participants' physical input, and also all the energies that they bring to bear as well. Don't be too concerned about the flashlight on the individual. Instead focus on the spotlight on the entire collaboration group."

Tabatha notes that some may be hesitant to collaborate because they are worried about being steamrolled or having ideas stolen. Tabatha has a refreshing and positive approach to this objection. She notes that whenever she approaches any project she has the best of intentions and love in her heart. She mentions being faith based and believing that what goes around comes around. She is solid in her belief that if someone does wrong to you it will come back to haunt them. She says, "Has something like that ever happened in my collaborations? Maybe, or maybe not; but if it has, the perpetrator has been taken care of. I don't worry about that."

Collaborations are important enough for growing our ideas that the fear of having one's ideas be stolen has not slowed down her zeal to collaborate and has not been a problem for her to date.

Tabatha mentions something that I think is a key part of learning, and that is being sure to be self aware. What kind of energy are we bringing to a project? Are we high-energy or more laid back? Are we making space for the other's ideas to be heard? Are we speaking up even if we are not usually the type of person who would speak up? A collaboration can be a great time to learn about our communication style and how we match with others. This will serve us through our outstanding collaborations, and may even help us in life in general.

Chapter Review

Let's personalize this for you and your business:

1) How open are you to giving your intuition a seat at the table when making decisions about collaboration alignment?

2) What has your experience been in the past in regards to your inner knowing? How does your inner knowing communicate with you?

3) Think of a time when you have listened to your inner knowing and the outcome was positive. What did you learn from that experience?

4) Think of a time when you failed to listen to your intuition, where the outcome was negative. What was your biggest take away from that situation?

Meditation

Take a deep breath for a count of four, hold for a count of four, and exhale for a count of four. Repeat for three times and feel yourself relax.

Take a few minutes to engage in quiet mind meditation. If you are an avid quiet mind meditator then set a timer for 15-20 minutes. If quiet mind meditation is new to you, then set your timer for seven minutes.

Focus on your breath. Breathe in for a count of four, hold for a count of four, exhale for a count of four. Imagine you are looking at a clear cloudless sky; there is nothing else in your field of vision except for blue clear sky.

Thoughts may intrude, and if they do, imagine they are clouds floating away out of your field of vision, and again focus on your breathing while imagining the beautiful cloudless sky.

Once your timer is done, and when it feels right for you, take out your journal and make notes focusing on how you can be in greater alignment in your collaborations.

Grow Smarter

Chapter 9

All In

There may appear to be overlap with the questions I ask myself ahead of a collaboration, however, it is all an important part of my process.

Once I've Asked, once I know the Alignment is good, then I have to focus on being All In. Firstly, asking the questions of myself: Am I all in? Am I bringing my best talents to the table? During this collaboration will I be working in my brilliance or just slogging away? And what about my mindset: Am I truly feeling there is abundance for all, or am I just paying lip service? Can I let go of the competition mindset and can I be open to abundance being delivered, perhaps, in unusual ways? Once I have answered these questions for myself then I can ask them of my partner.

Our LPL member, Dena Otrin, is a super smart lady. I have previously mentioned our conversation, however, she had more to share about collaborations. She shared another story, this time about a collaboration that she had that never got off the ground. Preface this by saying that she mentioned many of her collaborations that went swimmingly, but this one that never launched has the most to teach us. It's all about each person in the collaboration being all in. Dena notes that part of the plan for their collaborative event was that each person would have to do a share of the marketing.

That seems fair to you, right? Problem was that one of the members of the collaboration did not have the time that it would take to devote to the marketing portion of the plan. There was an opportunity, maybe at the beginning of the collaboration, to speak very frankly and clearly about expectations. That could have saved everyone a lot of time and effort, but at the end of the day, their event was not successful, and actually did not even get off the ground because all the partners were not putting out comparable levels of contribution.

Truly Feeling There is Abundance for All

I had the tremendous opportunity to talk with Susan Trumpler. She is a business coach and consultant, the founder of Unstoppable Women In Business, and the president of Beyond ROI. For Susan, the key to a successful collaboration is having a deep understanding of what it takes to support the success of another and a deep desire to provide that support. In order to do that, one has to truly feel as though there is abundance for all.

Susan mentions her process of developing a community avatar. We have all heard, I believe, of the ideal client avatar, but the community avatar takes it a step further, developing the profile of the type of group that it would be optimal for us to collaborate with. In developing this community avatar she asks:

- Who aligns with me, my business, and my culture?

- Who aligns with the way that I treat my community?

- Are we serving the same community in a little bit of a different way from each other?

- Do we have a tight connection?

- Do we share ideas about how the job should be done?

All that being said, in the story that Susan shared about one of her favorite successful collaborations, she notes that she didn't start by building the community avatar. In this case, she says that she started from the outside in.

The collaboration started because she met someone that she truly liked a lot. I know a lot of us can relate to that. Meeting someone who is so energetically aligned with our core values that we just know that we are meant to work together somehow. Susan continues that the other person's business did not have a lot to do with her established community avatar, but as they got to know each other the opportunities to work together began to show themselves more and more. They ended up collaborating by using something that was in the other person's business that Susan found would connect with members of her own community.

She mentions another story of collaborating with her dog's vet. Just getting into conversation and suddenly finding areas where their minds melded. It is obvious that she is open to the idea that abundance is available for all, and that collaborations can come from anywhere as long as you are open to it. She agrees that sometimes the most unexpected collaborations can end up being the best. Her final take away is to trust yourself. Listen to your gut and be open to receiving the collaborations and the abundance that are available for all of us.

Letting Go of the "Competition Mindset"

I had an outstanding time chatting with Suzanne McColl on LPL *Collaboration Conversations*. She is an EMDR therapist and works with entrepreneurs on their limiting beliefs to fast track their life and dreams. She brought to the fore a concept that we had skirted on other discussions, but with Suzanne we dove right in.

Suzanne explained that growing up she always was tuned in to the idea of helping others, but the idea of collaboration was not a concept that she learned early on. It was important for me to hear this from Suzanne because my experience growing up was so much different, and sometimes we can forget that all our experiences are unique.

She held back on collaborations in her business for a long time. She explained that she grew up in a family as one of seven kids and that individuality was not promoted. Suzanne helped her mom with the younger children. Who she was as an individual did not feel encouraged. When she was younger she was really quiet but as she grew up and grew into herself, as she got to know herself, she became more confident in speaking up, in holding her own, and in being a part of a collaboration.

Suzanne mentions that for many of us fear can be a deterrent from collaborating in business; the fear of not having something to offer, not being listened to, not being respected. Many people do not grow up with collaborating conversations. She notes that she certainly did not grow up that way, and that it took her a while to really learn the value of this. Now she has collaboration conversations with her children, asking for and valuing their opinions. She says that many people, because they don't grow up that way, do not know what collaboration is all about. They have learned a different path that tends to lead more to a competitive mindset. They have been sent that competitive message all their lives. Her kids are growing up learning the value of collaboration early on, and she believes that they will be enriched as a result.

Abundance Delivered in Unusual Ways

Lynn Gallant is a purveyor of fine clean-crafted wines and an active member of LPL and LPL inner circle. She shared on LPL *Collaboration Conversations* that she often sees collaborations where it might seem unusual or unexpected.

Lynn is a master collaborator, and her key reminders for us for successful collaborations are to focus on communication and creativity. She reminds us that conversations and communication need to continue throughout the collaboration. She further reminds us that confirming and affirming with each other during the entire process is very important. There is no such thing as too many conversations when working in collaboration.

Lynn shared a cute story about connecting with one of her clients who is a dog walker. They ended up collaborating to host a wine tasting event together – a wine tasting event especially for dog walkers. Certainly an unexpected idea, but it turned out to be an outstanding and successful event for both.

Another unexpected and successful collaboration was between Lynn and another of our LPL inner circle members, Robin Finney. Lynn and Robin collaborated to host a wine tasting and oracle card reading event which was an outstanding success. Lynn says that the collaboration started with both her and Robin being open to being creative and doing something that might be a bit unusual. Both were interested in putting on events that focused on fun self-care and bringing people together, and so they gave it a try.

It was a smashing success. Lynn mentioned that when she was inviting her clients, some did not know anything about oracle cards, but were interested in showing up to see what new exciting thing Lynn had to introduce them to. For Robin, her invitees did not know much about organic clean-crafted wine but if Robin was involved, they would absolutely show up. Based on the success of this event, they are now scheduling more of these events, and even joked in our interview that they would be interested in inviting even more collaborators to play.

Chapter Review

Let's personalize this for you and your business.

1) What has your approach been to collaboration projects? Have there been instances where you have held back? If you have what were your reasons? Fear of being steam rolled? Fear of having your ideas taken? Some other reason?

2) What is your single biggest take away from this chapter?

3) How can you apply this take away to your business and your collaborations to ensure that, going forward, both you and your collaboration partners are all in?

Meditation

Take a deep breath for a count of four, hold for a count of four, and exhale for a count of four. Repeat for three times and feel yourself relax.

Take a few minutes to engage in quiet mind meditation. If you are an avid quiet mind meditator then set a timer for 15-20 minutes. If quiet mind meditation is new to you, then set your timer for seven minutes.

Focus on your breath. Breathe in for a count of four, hold for a count of four, exhale for a count of four. Imagine you are looking at a clear cloudless sky; there is nothing else in your field of vision except for blue clear sky.

Thoughts may intrude, and if they do, imagine they are clouds floating away out of your field of vision, and again focus on your breathing while imagining the beautiful cloudless sky.

Once your timer is done, and when it feels right for you, take out your journal and make notes focusing on how you can be ALL IN with regards to your collaborations.

Grow Smarter

Chapter 10

Assignment

I admit it. I know how to do a lot of things. If you are in business as a solopreneur, you learn how to do a lot of tasks purely out of necessity. I know how to build a website, how to troubleshoot a possessed printer, and even how to clean the office bathrooms, but I would have to say that none of these things is my area of brilliance. When I'm entering into a collaboration, it can be tempting for me to invite myself to be the "do it all," but truly, that serves no one, and it certainly does not serve the collaboration project. For me, letting go of the need to be in control, and allowing each member to work in her brilliance while I work in mine, is a key to success that should not be overlooked. That brings us to discussing Assignment, making sure that each person in the collaboration is working in her brilliance as much as is possible.

Bringing Our Best Talents to the Table

During my collaboration conversation with Financial Architect Jackie Baldwin, I asked her what her definition was of collaboration and she went right into the idea of assignment; the idea that when we get together we bring resources. She clarifies that by resources, she means people who are specialists in different areas. She teaches us that when we each work in our own expertise, the client wins, the project wins, and we also win. It brings a richness to her client interactions because she can bring to her clients so much more than if she were working on her own. If we stay in our own tiny box we never grow. She likens a collaboration to ingredients coming together to make a delicious dish. She advises that we keep our minds open, think of what the other person does, and how that can serve our clients.

She mentions the example of working with clients on their financial goals, and drawing in the expertise of family law or elder law attorneys or even drawing on the expertise of other financial advisors that may be specialized in different areas from hers. She notes the example that she is licensed to write Medicare insurance but whenever she is working on that area with a client she always brings in an advisor that specializes in that area. She confirms that having a collaboration ensures that there are experts available in all the required fields.

Jackie mentioned an upcoming collaboration event that she has with an unlikely duo of collaborators. As I mentioned, Jackie is in finance and the event that she is planning is going to be hosted with a breast health expert and Carol, the woman who sells fine women's undergarments. At first blush, this may not at all seem like a possible collaboration, but they have made it work well in the past and are looking forward to their next event because they have been so successful in the past. Jackie says the key to their success lies in their sharing at the very beginning their visions and expectations. Communicating well about what the responsibility of each person will be is paramount to success. For example, in marketing the event, what is each person's responsibility? This is communicated clearly and at the beginning of the project.

Jackie goes on to reinforce the idea of the importance of communication and of being up front in the beginning. She says, "Do not assume." Her cautionary tale is about a collaboration she had with an attorney that she brought into the collaboration to focus on the long-term care side of things. She assumed that the attorney knew all of the areas of financial services that she offered, but she was wrong. She points out that the failing was that this was not clearly communicated at the beginning. The attorney went ahead and referred clients to another advisor for investing advice, which is, in fact, included in the services that Jackie offered to the collaboration. It was, however, not explicitly stated in the beginning, and, as a result, there was a gap in knowledge. Jackie says poor communication or a breakdown in communication is the number one reason that collaborations may not work. She suggests outlining things in an email, just so there is something in writing that can be referred to in the future. She also is a strong proponent of planning meetings.

I asked Jackie her opinion on getting collaboration partners to sign contracts. Jackie responded that we should think of a contract as a friendship preservation device. She advises that we should always have one especially when there is money involved. I absolutely agree with Jackie. The collective wisdom from all the women interviewed is: Collaborations gone wrong can wreck relationships. Have discussions and clear agreements from the beginning.

Working in Our Brilliance

Kristi Sullivan is a recovering marketer, Human Design expert, self-care guru, and yogi. She comes to us from the world of non-profit and is now working with female entrepreneurs to help them prioritize self-care. She joined us on LPL *Collaboration Conversations* and is someone with whom I have had successful collaborations in the past. I remember Kristi participating in one of the very first retreats that I hosted. I focused on the transformation and Kristi hosted the yoga portion. It went swimmingly; it was a memorable event, and now many years later sometimes friends who were part of that beautiful experience ask us about when we will get together in a collaboration like that again.

Assignment

Talking with Kristi truly brought out the importance of being open to what is available and working in your brilliance. She defines collaboration as a way of using leverage. She explains that coming from a background in non-profit, where budgets were small, collaborations were not only welcomed but almost expected. In that industry, co-promoting, sharing, and working together are the order of the day, and they fully realize they can do more, go farther, and stretch their dollars when they work together.

Kristi has shifted her field, but her commitment to collaboration remains as strong as ever. She is an expert in Human Design, and so she approaches the idea of collaboration from the point of view of considering each person's Human Design type. We talked about the optimal collaboration, and used the analogy of a road trip. In this analogy the Human Design type called the manifester is able to come up with the creative idea for what to do, where to go, and get us started on this journey. The Human Design type called the generator is the engine of the car. We are getting nowhere without the engine that drives our projects and gets us from point A to B. The Human Design type known as the projector is the navigation. Without someone pointing us in the right direction we could go nowhere fast or drive ourselves right off a cliff. Last, but not least, the Human Design type called the reflector is likened to the gauges of the vehicle telling us when we are operating at peak performance and providing warnings for us when we are not. In collaboration, when everyone is working in their brilliance, it is truly like a well-oiled machine, and may not even feel like work at all.

I asked for an example of a collaboration that Kristi has had that turned out successfully beyond her initial expectations, and she, with no hesitation, pointed to a recent collaboration that formed out of her and four other women who were part of a mastermind group. They came together to mastermind, and left as collaborators. It was not initially obvious that these women would collaborate. Kristi is in self-care and the other women are in energy, mindset, and marketing; one is a strategic business coach; one is a fashion stylist, and one is a coach who teaches public speaking.

They developed a collaborative partnership called POW 5 which focused on empowering women. It developed into a 5-week speaking series which they delivered online for the Community Renewal Team. They are now working together on a collaborative book project which will be available very soon.

Kristi says the key to the success of this collaboration is that they brought together synergistic energies. They all realized that they could do and be more together. She notes that a successful partnership is less about getting together to sell to

Assignment

someone and more about developing relationships with each other and with our clients.

Kristi's advice for us all is to:

- Be open to seeing the vastness of possibility.

- Don't force anything while being mindful of opportunities as they come up.

- Tune into your energy, and if the collaboration does not feel like it is a right fit it is OK to say "no."

- Understand your Human Design; you can even go so far as to create connection charts to see how you and another fit together.

- And, finally, she reminds us that for the majority it is best to make our decisions using the wisdom that comes from the body.

Chapter Review

Let's personalize this for you and your business.

1) What has your approach been to collaboration projects? Have there been instances where you have tried to do it all? If you have what were your reasons?

2) What would you consider your area or areas of brilliance, your best talents that you could offer a collaboration project? Make a comprehensive list. It could be the thing you do in your business, however, you could also include things that you do well and enjoy but that are not exactly your business. For example, I could bring knowledge of health care to a collaboration project, and I am also very good at *and* enjoy organizing, so I can bring that skill to our partnerships as well.

3) What is your single biggest takeaway from this chapter?

4) How can you apply this takeaway to your business and your collaborations to ensure that going forward both you and your collaboration partners are working in your zones of brilliance?

Meditation

Take a deep breath for a count of four, hold for a count of four, and exhale for a count of four. Repeat for three times and feel yourself relax. Take a few minutes to engage in quiet mind meditation. If you are an avid quiet mind meditator then set a timer for 15-20 minutes. If quiet mind meditation is new to you, then set your timer for seven minutes.

Focus on your breath. Breathe in for a count of four, hold for a count of four, exhale for a count of four. Imagine you are looking at a clear cloudless sky; there is nothing else in your field of vision except for blue clear sky. Thoughts may intrude, and if they do, imagine they are clouds floating away out of your field of vision, and again focus on your breathing while imagining the beautiful cloudless sky.

Once your timer is done, and when it feels right for you, take out your journal and make notes focusing on how you can be working in your zone of brilliance with regard to your collaborations.

Grow Smarter

Chapter 11

Applications and Resources

Technology, Delegation, Support

The other day I had a little bit of a quandary. I got into the office and was changing into my scrubs, when I realized that I was down to my last pair of scrub bottoms and that the drawstring had receded back into the waistband of the pants. It might surprise you, but this was not a problem I had ever experienced before. New problem right? Great opportunity to learn new things?

I changed back into my sweats and then engaged in mental gymnastics that would have impressed Einstein, as to how I was going to get the string back out. I tried quite a few ways to make it work but none were successful.

Now for those of you who are reading this who are seamstresses you know the answer to this quandary, but for me, forever the tomboy, the little girl who had always rebelled against anything to do with sewing, please believe me, I had no idea whatsoever.

After a few failed attempts, I finally decided that I

was going to have to get a pair of scissors, rip off the waistband and find the errant end. My plan was cut short by a simple conversation with Sandy. For those of you who don't know, Sandy is my right hand, my port in a storm, the reason I can do so much, because without her support and Manifesting Generator energy I would be one lost Super Projector.

Sandy is, among a million other things, a talented seamstress. She makes and sells cute bags, purses, and pocketbooks. We affectionately call her the bag lady. Why she was not my first go to is beyond me, because I know that living my optimal life means living the Grow Smarter pillars, and pillar #5 is APPLICATIONS: that includes tech resources, applications, delegation, and expert support.

I finally remembered to lean into the expert support that I had at my disposal. Sandy took the pants and then she did the one thing that I never imagined, and I almost screamed at her as she did it. It was so counter to everything I was thinking, my first thought when she did this was: OMG she has just made a bad situation worse. What did she do, what did she do...

I know you are on the edge of your chair waiting to find out...

She pulled the entire string out of the waistband. Now the waistband had no string. In my opinion this was the worst possible outcome, I was starting to sweat with the stress of this situation. Then she did something else that completely blew my mind. She MacGyvered it! In an office you use what you have available! She attached a paperclip to one end of the waist string, pushed it through the waistband and easily solved my problem. It took her less than a minute to fix something that I had been ruminating over, something that I had been struggling with by myself, for 20 full minutes. She did it quickly and easily, without even giving it any thought, and her method was so simple. The trick she used came to her as easily as breathing and yet it was way beyond anything that I had been able to think up on my own.

What are you hearing from this story? What is here for you? What lesson do *you* think we should all be drawing from this about Growing Smarter? (It's not taking up sewing as a hobby. LOL!)

I learned over a hundred lessons that day. I continue to be a work in progress and even though intellectually I know better, every day I just make my life a million times harder than it needs to be. I often have an "I can do everything," mentality. I power through and "get 'er done!" I work in areas that are not my brilliance and sometimes I forget to take advantage of the applications and resources. I forget to use the outstanding technology available to make my life flow easier. I forget to delegate assignments to the ones who have expertise in areas where I am lacking, and I forget that I have an outstanding support system, all standing ready to help, but needing me to ask. Is this just me? Can you relate?

That brings me to the final step in my collaboration process: Determining what resources I may need and taking note of what is available to me.

Often when we are in a collaboration, let's say we are collaborating with one other person, we can make the mistake of thinking that we have to do it all between the two of us. This could not be further from the truth. It's true that sharing the assignments makes sure each person is working in her sphere of brilliance, but what about the things that neither of you do well? This is a perfect opportunity to explore available technology, to delegate to another expert who may not have been part of the initial collaboration and to ask for support from your community of heart centered leaders. For every collaboration project that I get involved in, my list of questions always includes: What additional help can I take advantage of? What technology can make this easier? What support do I need and who can I delegate to?

I speak to female founders and women in business almost every day. The feedback I get is that the struggles that I have had in my business are not unique. They share with me that being a woman in business can be hard. They explain that being a solopreneur can be lonely. Many of the business leaders that come to me complain that they are just not making enough money, not getting enough traffic, visibility and customers. They feel as though they are networking but not seeing true return-on-investment. Many have tried collaborations in the past and before learning the five pillars for success in collaboration, they have seen their efforts not go well at all. They want to be able to grow and scale their businesses. They want to have a safe place to discuss ideas, ask for resources and support and even collaboration.

Initially as the ideas for this chapter formed, I thought of sharing a list of apps and resources that have been helpful to me in the past. I thought of outlining helpful resources that range from software platforms that help us get organized, platforms for setting up and hosting our websites, training programs, events and memberships, sites that help us automate and up level our branding, marketing, email marketing and social media, sites for sourcing expert support, and of course novel uses of many of the social sites out there.

As I thought more, I realized that every collaboration is unique and any list I make will not be exhaustive. In addition, with the pace at which technology moves, by the time I complete my list of favorite apps, more and better ones will be available! It also came to me that one of the beautiful things about belonging to a community of heart centered leaders ready to offer support, is that they are indeed *ready to offer support*, ready to answer questions about resources that can help ease our way.

Based on that, I decided to approach this portion a little differently, and to share instead about the resources that are available in our collaboration focused community. I have mentioned Ladies' Power Lunch previously. Let me take this opportunity to formally invite you and to welcome you as part of our movement of heart centered business leaders. Want to join us? Go to Growsmarternotharder.com

If you have a question about growing your business, about available resources, about technology or applications you might not have considered, if you are looking to delegate or if you need expert support, posing your question in the Ladies Power Lunch forum is an outstanding first step. And there is more. The Ladies' Power Lunch group (LPL) can even be a great place to cultivate outstanding relationships with other leaders that may lead to THE collaboration that could change your business forever.

I truly believe in the principles of Grow Smarter. I've seen the benefits first hand manifesting in my business and to be honest in all areas of my life. I have learned that intentionally aligned support brings a life of ease and flow and that is why in our LPL group we have one main rule: WE INTENTIONALLY SUPPORT EACH OTHER. It's noteworthy that we are not supporting each other because we are expecting something in return. We are engaging in a new paradigm that seems outrageous in business: just supporting each other because we exist and because we can. Crazy. Mind-blowing. Effective.

In our LPL community we see daily the results of coming together with this idea in mind. Together we prove that the power of the collective is greater than the sum of her parts. Remember the new math of $1 + 1 > 2$? We see magic showing up when two or more aligned minds get together. Ideas that we would not have had access to on our own show up with speed and accuracy, with the results of greater income and immpact for all.

In our community we prove that there is room for every single one of us to be successful. So what if you are a coach in a room of 500 coaches? There are about 7.77 Billion humans on earth. It's probably just me, but I think we can all find a few people to fill a practice! Competition is just a mental construct. The reason we believe in it so deeply is that this way of being has been the one subscribed to by society for generations. Let us draw our line in the sand here. Let us change the paradigm from crushing the competition to collaboration for success. You do not have to fail in order for me to succeed.

One more thing, this is where I get a little push back sometimes, but it is something that we prove daily in our LPL community: Struggle is optional. This goes against everything we have been taught. Well, at least what I learned. There is a Jamaican Proverb that translates loosely, "If you want good, your nose has to run." This suggests that achieving anything worthwhile requires stress and strain. Pick a culture, any culture, and you can find a similar saying or proverb. These are the sayings and knowings that we all learn at an early age. Ideas that are instilled into the fibre of our beings. Perhaps our ancestors had difficult times, and from a well-meaning place, passed these sayings on to help us to be resilient. There is tremendous value in resilience... and there is also tremendous value in leaning into the power of the collective and taking advantage of the support it provides.

The Grow Smarter principles, the foundation upon which Ladies' Power Lunch is built, promise to help us increase our income and our impact in our businesses, but it goes further than that. Growing smarter helps us live our optimal lives, helps us not just make more money with ease and flow, and helps us make deep and meaningful connections with like minded collaborators who truly have our best interest at heart.

The Grow Smarter Principles

- We want to grow, but we do not necessarily have greater energy or resources at our disposal.

- The traditional way is to use more force, do more, work harder, push through, just do it, drive, strive, push, grab, by any means necessary.

- My experience is that that approach just leads to overwork, overwhelm, burnout and lackluster results.

- We have all heard about attraction, and letting the universe work through us, and that also might feel a bit too passive and may provide inconsistent results.

- With the power of the collective at our back however, we can grow our income and impact without the efforting and with consistency and with the absolute knowing that all is happening, not to us, but for us.

The Five Pillars to Grow Smarter

1) **Ask:** Ask your inner guidance what your next step should be. In what way the collective can support you. Take time to gain clarity on your goals, dreams, and boundaries.

2) **Alignment:** Check in on your alignment and if there is a collaboration partner, check on their alignment as well. What is inner knowing saying about existing opportunities? Is there trust? Is there openness to what is available and what is possible? Is there openness to learning new lessons and open channels of communication?

3) **All In:** Are you all in? Is your partner all in? Do you get that there is abundance for all? Have you let go of the competitive mindset? Are you open to abundance showing up in any possible way?

4) **Assignment:** Is each partner focused in her area of brilliance, bringing her best talents to the table?

5) **Applications and Resources:** Don't expect to do everything and do not expect your collaboration partner to either. What support will you need? What specialized personnel will you need? How about non-human-resources?

Applications and Resources

What kinds of software, apps, technology, learning resources like books, podcasts, do you need? Posing your questions in the LPL group can be an outstanding way to harness the power of the collective and indeed grow smarter.

Grow Smarter

Chapter 12

Collaborate to Get Visible

If you are reading this book and you have gotten this far, then you are probably open to discussing collaboration to grow your impact and income in your specific business and this opportunity may be the one you have been looking for. I invite you to read on.

The Power Of The Collective Is Greater Than The Sum Of Her Parts.

I know it and so do you.

You have an amazing message to share with the world, right? But does it seem like the world is listening?

You're pretty sure you know you have what it takes, right?

You've done the inner work AND the outer work on yourself and your business, haven't you?

You believe in your talent and your ability to be a lightworker and shine your beautiful light.

And have you noticed that when you get with the right clients that it's like a symphony?

The problem is, you need a greater reach, you need a platform to get your message out there. And, truth be told it's just frustrating not having the impact or the income that you know you could.

(WARNING: This is only for you if you are ready to make the QUANTUM LEAP TO THE NEXT LEVEL OF LEADERSHIP. If you are not ready, that's OK, just don't read any further. But if leading your movement is part of your five year plan, then I invite you to read on. This is the sign you have been waiting for.)

I hate to sound cliche, but you are not alone. *Been there, done that, bought the t-shirt!* I'm a recovering researcher, y'all! I left my career in corporate where all I had to do was show up and do my job amazingly well and all the accolades, promotions, and financial remunerations would show up.

I had a crisis of conscience that led me down a totally different career path. (Story for another day!) Fast forward through me going back to school, studying all the things, and becoming a holistic physician and optimal life coach.

When I started my business, I knew I had something fabulous to offer. I learned that one of the best ways to use my time was to meet prospective clients in large groups through speaking engagements. I was so excited to put my message out there and then...*crickets*.

Has that ever happened to you? Have you joined all the networking groups, only to find yourself networking with people who aren't properly motivated to help you grow? People who only pay lip service to the concept of supporting each other? Have you been a speaker at event after event, to gain "exposure," but found that many of those events did little to truly explode your reach?

That was my story too. I spoke everywhere they would have me, but that did little to grow my list or my practice. I did all the other things too: website, mail campaigns, networking, email newsletter, blog, social media, you name it, and I've probably done it and could teach you to do it well. And I did get a *few* amazing clients, but for the most part, it felt like I was shouting into the wind. If you've read this far, I'm guessing you are probably a lot like me.

You are most likely an established entrepreneur, you probably transitioned into light work from a more traditional career path. You are great at what you do. You LOVE the work you do. You have spent the time working on *and* in your business and now *it's time to take it to the next level.*

"What does your intuition tell you about your true potential?"

"Do you care about your passion enough to stand up and be the leader the world needs?"

"Are you ready to do it NOW?"

You just need to get your message heard by the right people. You just need to connect with your community so that you can serve the wonderful souls that you were sent here to co-create with. And that will mean that you can live the life you want on your terms. That will mean that you will achieve the satisfaction of helping more of the people that you are meant to help, and it will also mean that you will be able to achieve the goals that you have that are JUST FOR YOU.

But how????

It would be amazing if exposure came at the snap of a finger, but the truth is, for most of us it doesn't. Most people spend a lot of time, effort, and might I say dollars, trying to figure out the formula for being seen, growing, and taking their businesses to the level that their true potential suggests they could.

I'm going to just say here that trying the same old tired strategies would most likely leave you exactly where you are right now or at least not very much more advanced. As we mentioned earlier, it has been said that insanity is doing the same thing and expecting different results.

What if we approached this differently? What if we harness the power of the collective? A rising tide lifts all boats, so why don't we approach this collaboratively and all grow together?

You may have been a member of Ladies Power Lunch for a while, or maybe you have at least heard of LPL. If you have, then you know that our number one guiding principle is INTENTIONALLY supporting each other.

The LPL Quantum Leadership Circle takes this support and makes it intentional so that you grow, your business grows, and the people who are losing sleep at night because they are looking for someone just like you can find you.

Close your eyes... Imagine yourself being truly seen by YOUR ideal clients. Imagine having a community that intentionally and whole-heartedly supports YOUR visibility. Imagine taking your calling to the obvious next step with ease and grace. Imagine achieving the goals that you have that are just for you, with minimum effort and time.

If all of that truly happened, what would that make possible? How would your life change for the better?

Here's the FORMULA for getting on the fast track.

I'm going to give you my formula for visibility. It's amazing and it WORKS! It all starts with being seen and heard while becoming a part of a beautiful and supportive community.

1) Be seen and heard on big stages.

But wait, here's the thing. Hopping onto a big stage is not productive if you are not stage-ready. What this means is that you need to learn how to craft your talk that converts attendees into clients, and then the next phase is learning to deliver that talk. Then you need to learn how to get booked on the stages that will be meaningful for you.

You want to hone your message for greatest impact, and extend your reach as a national and international speaker, reaching at least 50,000 like minded women (and source-led men.) To do this you need to get booked on:

- Workshops

- Summits

- Retreats

2) Be seen and heard by publishing a bestselling anthology *and* a bestselling book.

Become a bestselling published author with your very own chapter in an anthology work. That's an amazing starting point. The next step is becoming a bestselling author of your solo work. In many cases you will have the option of including audio, e-book, and print versions. I say take advantage of all of the options as different people like consuming media in different ways. Some people prefer to listen to books, some like reading on their devices, and some people love the good old paper books and won't read anything else!

- Print

- Ebook

- Audiobook

3) Be seen and heard on media channels.

Media trends show that video and podcasts are the wave of the future. Take advantage of these trends to extend your reach beyond your following. But wait! First you need to get media-ready and then explode your audience using a podcasting network affiliation.

There are many platforms and you need to be on all of them: Apple podcasts, Amazon, Stitcher, Spotify and other platforms. Also be sure to have a robust YouTube channel. Remember YouTube is the number two search engine in the world! If you want to be seen you have to be there. And one more thing, not only host your own podcast, but also be a strategic guest on other podcasts.

- YouTube

- Amazon

- Apple podcasts, etc...

4) Mastermind with entrepreneurs who have similar growth goals.

Napoleon Hill was a strong advocate of the power of working together collaboratively vs. struggling to do it all alone! In his books *The Law of Success* and *Think and Grow Rich*, he advocated using the power of the collective to obliterate perceived obstacles and grow. Mastermind with a very small hand-picked group of high achieving and, most importantly, intentionally supportive women just like you.

Visibility grows as a result of employing these four simple visibility steps so take advantage of:

- Extending your reach, not just to anyone but to over 50,000 of the right kinds of people, the ones that you want to hear your message, and the ones that will be able to fill your practice and join your movement.

- Honing your public speaking skills. I'm pretty sure you are great at speaking and crafting your talk, but is your signature talk a million dollar talk? Will it wow your audience in a full stadium? Will it truly energize the people that you are meant to lead and support?

- Exploding all the ways that audiences can connect with you, from print to podcasts, thereby up-leveling your profile and allowing you to be seen as THE authority in your field and THE leader of your movement.

- Making a quantum leap into the leadership role you are made for, and that the world has been waiting for. You are going to be amazing, there is no doubt about that, but if you could fast-track your success, what would that make available to you?

- Having an opportunity to have the income that allows you to achieve the freedom and the things that you want that are just for you, while doing what you love and are passionate about.

- Being able to connect deeply with a small intimate group of hand-selected like minded souls who are committed to nurturing your dream.

"The dream you think could happen for you some day, could happen for you NOW!"

You could:

- Become a sought after speaker who converts attendees to clients from the stage!

- Become a bestselling author.

- Collaborate with other entrepreneurs just like you to become an LPL recommended provider

- Increase your reach by being a member of the LPL podcast network.

- Mastermind with other leaders to grow your reach and impact.

What do you want to do? It's all up to you. We are here to provide support!

This is an invitation to you.

Does the idea of the power of the collective supporting your life's work sound amazing for you?

Does supporting the dreams of your fellow light workers feel exactly like what we should be doing always?

Would you like to find the right group of women (and a few source-led men) who intentionally share this belief of rising together?

I invite you to apply to work with me and a handpicked group of industry leaders (because, well, collaboration!) to grow your impact and income. Will you go to our website and take it from there?

Go to:
https://www.growsmarternotharder.com/survey

My intention with sharing all this is to help heart centered entrepreneurs to live their optimal entrepreneurial lives. I'd love for you to truly have the kind of freedom in your businesses that you expected when you were newly minted. I'd love for you to increase your reach and your impact and to never have you worry about having enough clients again, ever. And I'd love for you to have the income that allows you to run your business in the way you want to, give back in the way your heart calls, and have the things that you want that are just for you. It's possible and it's not rocket science. The power of the collective and the art of collaboration can get you there. You can live your best entrepreneurial life. You get to choose.

Grow Smarter

About Dr. Davia H. Shepherd

Dr. Davia H. Shepherd is a holistic physician and master connector. A certified retreat leader and recovering researcher, she is celebrating almost 20 years in various areas of healthcare. She loves public speaking and is an international speaker and bestselling author. She helps female entrepreneurs live the best version of their lives in every area: health, business, relationships, finances. She leads transformational retreats, conferences, and Ladies' Power Lunch networking events. Davia lives in the suburbs in Connecticut with her outstanding husband, Wayne, two amazing miracle boys, Preston and Christian, and her mom, Phyllis.

Also by Dr. Davia H. Shepherd

Success in Any Season

Transformation 2020

Transformation 2020 Companion Journal

The Great Pause: Blessings & Wisdom from COVID-19

The Great Pause Journal

About Green Heart Living

Green Heart Living's mission is to make the world a more loving and peaceful place, one person at a time. Green Heart Living Press publishes inspirational books and stories of transformation, making the world a more loving and peaceful place, one book at a time.

Whether you have an idea for an inspirational book and want support through the writing process – or your book is already written and you are looking for a publishing path – Green Heart Living Press can help you get your book out into the world.

You can meet Green Heart authors on the Green Heart Living YouTube channel and the Green Heart Living podcast.

www.greenheartliving.com

Green Heart Living Press Publications

Success in Any Season

Redefining Masculinity

Your Daily Dose of PositiviDee

Transformation 2020

Transformation 2020 Companion Journal

The Great Pause: Blessings & Wisdom from COVID-19

The Great Pause Journal

Love Notes: Daily Wisdom for the Soul

*Green Your Heart, Green Your World:
Avoid Burnout,
Save the World and Love Your Life*

CPSIA information can be obtained
at www.ICGtesting.com
Printed in the USA
BVHW051124270721
613006BV00002B/202